Gardens to Visit
Lower North Island

Alison McRae

David Bateman

For our grandchildren Vanessa, Tim, Ben and Sam

Author's Note: While every effort is made to supply accurate information with regard to the style and visiting details of any garden, the nature of gardening and people means that this information changes very rapidly. The author and publisher take no responsibility for changes to the garden entry and advise garden visitors to check important details before visiting any garden.

First published in 1989 by David Bateman Ltd, Tarndale Grove, Albany Business Park, North Shore City, Auckland, New Zealand
Revised edition 1990, 1992, 1994, 1995, 1996

ISBN 1 86953 296 1

Printed in Hong Kong by Colorcraft
Jacket design by Errol McLeary

Poverty Bay

Nigel and Avianne Faram,
"Parihohonu", Main Road, Otoko, R.D.2, Te Karaka.Tel/Fax:(06) 862 3459
A hill-top garden set above an adjacent stand of native bush, Parihohonu has a unique view. The tops of the big trees can be looked down on and many native birds observed. The garden is a mixture of trees, shrubs and rose beds. One feature is a wide spreading cherry tree; another is a pergola covered with scarlet bougainvilleas. One can sit in here and, as Avianne says, look at a very special view of the world.
Garden can be visited all year. Teas available. Groups, please phone in advance.

Rosemary and Graham Johnson,
"The Willows", Waipaoa R.D.1, Gisborne.   **Tel:(06) 862 5605**
 A number of fine mature trees are the dominant feature here at The Willows; copper beech, oak, cedar, tilia, Wellingtonias and some of the largest Tasmanian blackwoods to be seen in New Zealand. Extensive lawns flow from a flat area down a hillside where there is a reflection lake and onto more flat areas dotted with specimen trees and masses of daffodil bulbs; a wonderful sight in spring. The long drive has a mixed line of colourful trees and shrubs, quite a number of these are camellias. Elsewhere, beds of old-fashioned roses, perennials and bulbs blend with blossom trees and a collection of climbers. Delightful rural views can be enjoyed all around the garden, which is pretty spring and autumn.
Visits by appointment. Entry fee for groups.

Kay and Peter Tomlinson,
Ormond, R.D.1, Gisborne.   **Tel:(06) 862 5555**
A long section in an orchard growing area with a microclimate that is home to a number of temperate plantings. Some rare and special specimens can be seen. Over a

3

small pond grows a very large weeping Japanese maple and along the road a line of jacarandas creates a special feature in early summer. Camellias, conifers, magnolias and maples mix with beds of perennials, bulbs and old roses. An easy-walking, interesting country garden with something to see all year.

Visits by appointment.

Lesley and Dean Witters,
"Waiohika", Waimata Valley Rd, Gisborne.   **Tel:(06) 867 4670**
Waiohika was built in 1920 by a Napier architect, Louis Hay. He modelled it on the "Little House", Pretoria, Illinois, designed by Frank Wright. Fine specimens of mature trees are a feature surrounding an historic house which is a copy of a Frank Llloyd Wright design. To complement the large dwelling, the garden and large sweeping lawns are framed with 100-year-old Wellingtonias, jacarandas, *Magnolia grandiflora, Gordonia,* titoki, nikau palms, liquidambars, pohutukawa, puka, grevillea and maples, to name a few. Hahas are placed so as not to spoil the lovely rural views. Plantings of camellias, modern roses and lavender hedges with perennial beds, small ponds where flat local stone has been used in landscaping, and a small lake with bog plantings add to the overall delightful and colourful picture. Rustic pergolas support roses and frame patios designed around family living. More subtropical palms and plants are planned around the lily pond area, in contrast to the more formal front garden which is edged in *Buxus sempervirens* hedges. Native bird song is a constant pleasure.

Visits by appointment. Entry fee. 6 km from city boundary and close by Grays Bush Reserve, which also has a lookout providing a wonderful view over the Gisborne countryside. Morning and afternoon teas can be provided for groups by prior arrangement.

Mary and Spencer Bush,
"Karaka", Ngatapa, R.D.2, Gisborne.   **Tel:(06) 863 9868**
A rural garden on several levels, Karaka has trees planted within the house section and a great variety in the surrounding paddocks thus creating a park-like section with a visual extension. Flowerbeds are a mixture of old roses, perennials and a host of bulbs. A shady bog garden with a bridge has lots of leafy and foliage plantings. Paths and steps to all areas are easy walking. Spring is very colourful and autumn brilliant for the leaf display.

Visits by appointment for groups only. Teas by arrangement.

"Eastwoodhill Arboretum",
On the Rere-Ngatapa Rd (35 km west of (Gisborne).
Occupying around 64 hectares, Eastwoodhill has the largest collection of Northern Hemisphere trees in the Southern Hemishpere; comprising over 3000 trees, shrubs and climbers. Included are all the popular garden species; camellias, rhododendrons, azaleas, maples, beech, magnolias, ash, birch, oak, lime, cherry and peach, and many conifers such as spruce, juniper, pine, cedar, fir, ginkgo and many, many more.

Spring brings mass displays of naturalised daffodils and early blossoms; in autumn the park is almost as colourful. Semi-formal gardens surround part of the homestead and there are lots of perennials, bulbs, ground covers and foliage plants such as hostas and hydrangeas. The whole area is accessible on foot and many of the tracks pass ponds and lakes, opening up new vistas at every corner. Many of the trees are named. Ground, tree and water birds are plentiful and the chorus is endless. Whether a tree-lover or a plant-fancier, there is something for everyone here year-round and time must be allowed to enjoy it all.

Open daily, 10 a.m. to 4 p.m. At other times by appointment. Closed Good Friday and Christmas Day. Groups welcome but prior notice would be appreciated. A guided tour can be provided by prior arrangement. Entry fee. For further information, write to the Curator, Mr G. Clapperton, R. D. 2, Gisborne, or telephone (06) 863 9800.

Nick and Pat Seymour,
"Wenslydale", R.D.3, Gisborne.   Tel:(06) 862 2697

A pretty country garden on gently sloping and flat areas, Wenslydale relies on mixed plantings for seasonal displays. Camellias start the early spring flowering, followed by azalea mollis and blossom trees. Next come the perennials and roses, modern and old-fashioned. Pat has a small collection of orchids and cyclamens in a shelterhouse.

Visits by appointment from September through to November only. Morning, afternoon teas and light lunches available by prior arrangement for groups. Entry fee.

Peter and Norma Murphy,
"Panikau", Whangara, R.D.3, Gisborne.   Tel:(06) 862 2683

Panikau is a very large country garden, semi-formal in design and with a number of prominent features. An enclosed garden on one side of the house has terraced beds planted with modern and old-fashioned roses and mixed perennials; another side has an enclosed playground. In front, is a large split level lawn edged with a haha; over this is a magnificent view toward Mount Hikurangi. Probably the most prominent feature is a massive pergola made of local stone, as are all the walls that form the enclosures. This very long and wide pergola supports many different climbers, including jasmine, wisteria, mandevilla, thunbergia, the wanga wanga vine, vitis and New Zealand's own tecomanthe. Another part of the front area is given over to an extensive rock garden with plantings of bulbs, perennials and ground covers. Almost surrounding the whole garden are mature trees, some up to 100 years old; redwoods, cedars, oaks, elms and liriodendrons, to name a few. Around the farm, Peter has also planted patches with many species and varieties of trees that he has grown himself from seeds and cuttings. Please allow time to see all this.

Visits by appointment. Entry fee. Garden plants for sale.

Ian and Sue Fraser,
"Hikatu", Whangara, R.D.3, Gisborne.   Tel:(06) 862 2850

Here is a true 'gardener's garden' with different and interesting corners everywhere. One section is a cool restful woodland area where shade-loving plants thrive. Long terraced gardens, mass planted with perennials and bulbs, frame the front of the house. Several small ponds feature; these are edged with bog plants, hostas, irises and primulas. Roses, both modern and old-fashioned, grow throughout. Trees surround the section and are of a mixed variety but include a collection of camellias and magnolias. An extended area which began at the beginning of the '90s is a tranquil and restful place; no room for lawns, paths throughout and, as Sue says, rather wild. A white garden, fairy garden, mixtures of herbs and vegetables, archways of old climbing roses, camellias and some natives all blend together. Best time for viewing is October to December, although there is interest all year.

Visits by appointment. Morning & afternoon tea arranged for groups. Entry fee.

Miss M. Spencer,
"Welcombe", 463 Aberdeen Drive, Gisborne.   **Tel:(06) 867 3119**
This gentle two-level cottage garden is cultivated on biodynamic principles. It is very pretty, with masses of cottage plants as well as roses, herbs, trees and shrubs. Scented plants are also important here. Margaret's design philosophy is that we must seek Nature's lines all the time, and in her garden flowing contours blend all the different corners together; she has used logs for plants to drape over instead of stakes, this being more natural.
Visits by appointment.

Mr Dick Richardson,
No. 1 Riverside Rd, Gisborne.   **Tel:(06) 868 8883**
In this cool, pleasant woodland garden an unusual feature is a viewing platform over-looking the Waimata River. There are lots of foliage plantings, also collections of rhododendrons, camellias and magnolias as well as semi-tropical species such as banana, palms, pawpaw, hibiscus, vireya rhododendrons and cycads.
Visits by appointment.

Owen and Nan Poole,
"Witsend", 30 Island Rd, Gisborne.   **Tel:(06) 867 5554**
Roses take centre stage in this 0.2-hectare urban garden. Modern varieties fill beds bordered by miniatures and also feature in beds combined with appropriate perenni-als. Some of the roses here are Nan's own, propagated from imported stock. A mixed shrubbery of camellias and other trees adds variety to the landscape. Best viewing time for the roses is October and November.
Visits by appointment.

Liz and Mark Karalus
"Karalus Gardens", Papatu Road, Manatuke, Gisborne. Tel: (06) 862 8745
Old-fashioned cottage plantings fill the flower beds surrounding this house on a level section. Many David Austin roses in the beds and over archways, herbs and lavenders feature. An attractive central garden designed in a semi-formal pattern is planted around an old house foundation and the surplus broken concrete, where the colour is a mixture of white, blues, greys and green. Alongside is a formal herb garden with clipped lavender and rosemary hedging. A new area of natives is under development and on a lower level is a plantation of mixed eucalyptus reached by a wide grass pathway edged with many shrubs, natives and leafy plantings. Garden ornaments appear throughout. A large area is also under development for commercial herb growing. A nurs-ery has a selection of roses, herbs perennials, shrubs and garden ornaments.
Open for public viewing Labour Weekend to 30 November, 10 a.m. to 5 p.m. Friday, Saturday, Sunday only. Other times by appointment. Entry fee.

Joan and Paul Pollock,
"Highgate", Private Bag, Gisborne.   **Tel:(06) 862 8435**
 Highgate is fortunate in that its naturally sheltered site, coupled with volcanic soil, near frost-free conditions and sloping terrain, enables many unusual and interesting plants to be grown. A backbone of established 60-year-old oaks and chestnuts, and a restored 700-square metre homestead, enhance the wilderness setting in which tradi-

tional English features such as a bluebell hillside, cherry walk, old-rose arbour and azalea dell grow side by side with tropical palms, bougainvilleas and hibiscus. A nursery growing and selling mandarin and avocado trees supports the property. Experimental plantings of tropical guavas, sapotas and loquats are among the different types of fruit grown.

Visits by appointment. Entry fee. Teas or lunches can be provided for groups by prior arrangement.

Rodney and Sarah Faulkner,
"Wairakaia Station", Private Bag, Gisborne.   Tel:(06) 862 8607
A long drive through an avenue of mature oaks, elms, plane trees and ash trees leads to this hillside garden, which enjoys superb rural and sea views. A semi-circular pergola covered with roses, thunbergias and other climbers shades a peaceful rest area. Long stone walls, a white rose bed and a collection of Malaysian rhododendrons are other features in this garden. A large dry bank is mass planted with perennials. There are about 4 hectares surrounding the house garden with trees and shrubs of many varieties.

Visits by appointment.

Roger and Carol Gillingham,
"Rimuhau", Waerenga-0-Kuri, Gisborne.   Tel:(06) 867 8479
Large overhead trees shelter a woodland area planted in camellias, species rhododendrons, magnolias, azaleas and lots of shade-loving ground covers, perennials and bulbs. Elsewhere there are beds of perennials, bulbs and masses of old-fashioned roses. Two old roses, "New Dawn", climb over the front of the house providing a great splash of pink over spring. All of Carol's plantings are colour coordinated and fragrance is also considered when choosing plants. A collection of clematis, a laburnum walk, a small corner with mahonias and the vege patch are other interesting additions.

Garden available to visit most days by appointment.

Simon and Rosie Spence,
"Taaheke", Waerenga-0-Kuri, Gisborne.   Tel:(06) 863 7077
Sited on gently sloping land and also including a steep bank, the garden at Taaheke is still developing. One area is mass planted in perennials, old roses, ground covers and a variety of trees and shrubs, including rhododendrons and mollis azaleas. This creates a very pretty picture during spring and early summer. There is a wide lawn area, partly edged with a haha, and from here one gets a splendid view of mixed tree specimens planted in a paddock.

Visits by appointment.

Bob and Anne Berry,
or Kevin and Diane Playle,
"Hackfalls Arboretum", P.O. Box 2, Tiniroto.   Tel:(06) 863 7091/(06) 863 7083
This is a unique collection of trees in an area of 20 hectares, and some notable trees are to be seen. Examples of half the oak species of the world can be found here and certainly the best collection of Mexican oaks outside of Mexico. There are many other species such as beech, maple, chestnut, birch, prunus, alder, eucalyptus, magnolia, rhododendron, populus and willow. Large lakes and dams, surrounded by plantings, are home to many waterfowl. One can wander for hours over rolling hills to observe

the groups of trees and specimens. The homestead garden has many unusual herbaceous and alpine treasures, indluing a fine collection of natives, and a small pond and bulb plantings. A nursery set amongst the garden has plants for sale. The best time to visit is spring, when flowering blossoms are magnificent, and autumn, when the turning leaf colour is spectacular. Please allow time to see and enjoy.

Open all year, visitors welcome by appointment. Picnics. Entry fee, children free.

Hawke's Bay

Margaret and Ian Maxwell,
"Paeroa", P.O. Box 45, Nuhaka.   **Tel:(06) 837 9709**
Large level lawns with curved beds on either side frame wide views in this garden. A
feature is a semi-formal rose bed of mostly old roses, some of which have been grafted
by Margaret. A grove of ginkgo trees is a focal point of entry. A cool woodland area has
a wall along one side made from local stone. Around the perimeter of this garden are
mixed conifers and deciduous trees. Camellias also feature in the garden collection.
Visits by appointment.

John and Jan Bayly,
"Tahaenui Station", Private Bag 100, Wairoa.   **Tel:(06) 837 8707**
Here a large rural garden has been developed on different levels. It is surrounded by
mature trees, and very large Norfolk pines form an avenue to its wide sweeping lawns.
The flower beds are massed with old-fashioned roses, perennials and bulbs.
*Visits by appointment. Entry fee. Available to garden groups and bus tours only
during the months of October, November and December.*

Jill and Bob Haynes,
"Waihua Station", P.O. Box 17, Wairoa.   **Tel:(06) 837 7800**
A sub-tropical country garden with mature trees, which include jacaranda, puriri, pohutukawa and Norfolk pine; also shrubs such as hibiscus, gardenia and frangipani. A
large clump of Queensland lilies is a magnificent sight when in flower. Flower beds
contain perennials, bulbs and old roses, the lawns here are flat and wide. This garden
is home to many native birds.
*Visits by appointment. Morning and afternoon teas or light lunches by prior
arrangement. Toilet available.*

Judith and Chris Redmond,
"Burnleigh", R.D.1, Wairoa.   **Tel:(06) 837 7843**
A hillside garden, Burnleigh suffers from dryness at times. Its driveway leads through
an avenue of agapanthus, silver birches and a collection of camellias. The flower beds
are massed with perennials, old-world roses and companion plants. New plantings of
native trees and shrubs add interest.
   Visits by appointment. Entry fee. The garden is open October and November only.

"Coastal Gardens"

Heather and John Dean,
"Mangarara", P.O. Box 100, Nuhaka.   **Tel:(06) 837 8738**
This hillside garden emphasises trees and shrubs. One part is intensively planted in
conifers and there are a number of species and varieties from the tall to the low and
spreading. In the northern temperate section one finds a variety of deciduous trees
(with briliiant autumn colour); this area blends into Australian and South African
plantings. Here, flowering, fruiting and berry trees can be seen. Natives have a place;
these shelter some of the sub-tropical species: banana, pawpaw, cassava and guava.
Dotted throughout are bulbs and perennials which add colour and interest, as does
extensive stone work. Beyond the house section there are farm forestry plantings. Pottery for sale. Appearing throughout are bulbs, perennials and attractive stone work.
   Spring is colourful while autumn has brilliant leaf display. Home stays for two by
arrangement. Garden open to public daily Labour Weekend to end November, 9 a.m.
to 5 p.m. Other times by appointment, spring to leaf fall. Mangarara is closed
Saturdays. Entry fee

Rose-Marie and Roger Bremner,
"Bremdale", Wai St, P.O. Box 58, Nuhaka.   **Tel:(06) 837 8729**
Bremdale — or "The Garden of Eden" as it is affectionately known — is an intensively
planted cottage garden, rather romantic and intimate, developed in rooms, alcoves and
corners. Masses of old-fashioned roses, perennials, flowering herbs, trees, shrubs and
bulbs fill the whole garden. Many plantings reflect Rose-Marie's interest in dried flowers
and she has some special beds just for this purpose. Paved and grass walkways, lots of
seats, archways, pongas and stone work add interest. A wild garden, where self-seeding flowers can be seen amongst the grasses and fruit trees, adding another dimension.
Figures and statues dot the garden. The Bremners practise an organic policy in the
garden, orchard and farm. Doves, pigeons and peacocks call Bremdale home. A Flower
Barn is stocked full of dried flowers, mostly from the garden, and a number of Rose-
Marie's creations. New developing gardens surround a large pond, more rustic archways and some formal plantings. Roger makes manuka garden furniture and any design may be ordered for purchase. As this is a family garden, it is a place where visiting
children enjoy the atmosphere.
   Open Labour Weekend to the end of November daily, 9 a.m. to 5 p.m. Other times
usually open spring to leaf fall (look for open sign). Teas and luncheons available by
arrangement. Rose-Marie will holds seminars throughout the Eastlands area on all
aspects of floral art with natural materials and dried flowers. Toilets. Entry fee.

John and Elizabeth Powdrell,
"Opoho" — Heritage Trail ,
Bag 2012, Wairoa.   **Tel: (06) 837 7848 /Fax: (06) 837 7440**
A large pleasant coastal garden has been created here under sometimes trying conditions. The wide sweeping lawns are framed by well-grown trees and an area of woodland is full of cool-loving plants and flowering trees and shrubs. Flower beds of roses, perennials, bulbs and camellias are enhanced by limestone rock and water features. The entrance has a brightly welcoming garden which incorporates 'sculptures' of old tree stumps. It is a garden for all seasons with many interesting corners.

A nursery stocks many of the plants found in the garden. The garden is open daily from Labour Weekend to the end of November, 9 a.m. to 5 p.m. Other times — usually open from spring to leaf fall, arrangement preferred. Entry fee. Brochures available. Morning, afternoon tea and lunches for groups can be arranged

---

Rukautanu Forest Park, Waikoau, Hawke's Bay.
This is 16 hectares of planted forest, the work of the late Mr and Mrs H. R. Holt, Here you will find many groves of trees from all over the world mixing happily with natives. Examples are eucalyptus, redwood, Douglas fir, Japanese cedar, Corsican pine, Mexican pine, Tasmanian stringy bark, Alaskan sitka and Norwegian spruce. There are tracks, roadways and streams with bridges. Birds are plentiful all year round and planting here has taken into account their needs. Along the water edges and in the dark dells grow many different ferns, from the huge black pongas to small ground ferns. Early spring brings a mass display of daffodils through an avenue of Douglas firs on one side and Californian redwoods on the other; a stately introduction to a very worthwhile place to visit for anyone interested in trees and nature. The park is in the hands of a trust. It takes time to see it all.

For further information please contact Mr Peter Holt, c/o Post Office, Tutira, Hawke's Bay, or telephone (06) 839 7704.

John and Fiona Wills,
"Trelinnoe Park", Te Pohue, R.D.2, Napier.   **Tel:(06) 834 9703**
Situated just off the Napier to Taupo highway, Trelinnoe Park, A Garden of Landscape, covers 11 hectares and offers interest all the year round. Trees and shrubs, such as rhododendrons, azaleas, magnolias, conifers and camellias, combine with a collection of the warmer temperate varieties: jacarandas, vireya rhododendrons and bougainvilleas. An interesting collection of native ferns and trees includes pohutukawa. There are mass displays of bulbs in spring, and autumn is notable for the brilliant leaf colouring. Sweeping lawns, flower and rock gardens and easy-walking paths through woodland areas give year-round pleasure to visitors.

Park open every day 10 a.m. to 5 p.m. August until the end of May. Cafe open every day October, November and January; Thursday to Sunday September, April and May; weekends only December until Boxing Day, February and March. Entry fee. Cafe operates 10 a.m. to 5 p.m. and is open on all Public Holidays. Can be opened on request at other times. There are crafts for purchase.

Val and Don Organ,
"Cotswold", R.D.2, Te Pohue, SH5, Napier.   **Tel:(06) 834 9716**
Even though this large hillside garden is covered in snow at times, there is a wide variety of trees, shrubs and perennials to be seen. Wandering paths and steps wind throughout presenting delightful vistas at every turn. Masses of primulas, flag irises, ground covers, bulbs and blossom trees blend with rhododendrons, azaleas and conifers. A lake on a lower level is fed by a stream tumbling over stones and spanned by a long hump bridge. White swans, scoup doves and peacocks enjoy the garden's tranquillity. A cherry walk, archways, pergolas, many garden seats and clipped hedges are features. Bricks have been used for patio construction and local stone for raised beds and edgings.
   Garden available for visiting 7 days, October to May. Entry fee.

Patricia and Lloyd Smith,
"Brookbury Perennial Nursery and Cottage Garden",
Hale Road, Meeanee, Napier.   **Tel: (06) 834 4606**
A level lawn area has had beds developed around the outer perimeter for the display of masses of perennials. A pond is also a feature. Patricia has a nursery with plants for sale that can be seen in the garden.
   Open by appointment, September till February.

Botanical Gardens,
Napier Terrace, Spencer St, Napier.
These gardens, created in 1855, occupy a deep gully and there are concrete walkways and steps throughout. The large mature trees, many of which were brought to Napier by the captains of sailing ships, are of mixed plantings but look quite sub-tropical with a variety of palms, jacarandas, Norfolk pines, cycads, cacti and bougainvilleas. In 1874 the gardens were developed to include flower beds. Near the lower area there is a big grassed section with a waterway flowing through. Edged with damp-loving plants, this stream flows into a large pond. There is a lot of stonework on garden edges, banks and walls. An aviary nestles amongst tall trees.
   Accessible at all times. Toilets available.

Gavin and Jill Ebbett,
Kimpton Hills, R.D.3, Napier.   **Tel:(06) 844 4679**
Trees and shrubs are the main plantings in this large country garden. Extensive lawns have blossom trees, conifers, camellias, rhododendrons, a collection of the protea varieties, some natives and deciduous trees. Set in a basin and with dry conditions only the hardy species will grow. A long driveway lined with trees is an attractive entrance. Picnics in garden welcome, ample seating.
   Visits by appointment.

Rose Gardens, Kennedy Park,
Storkey St, Napier.
Kennedy Park has an oblong area which is framed on one side with a large trellis supporting climbing roses. In front are beds of bush roses, edged with begonias. Many beds have been formed into patterns of mixed colours combined with one colour bush roses. Dotted throughout are weeping standard roses. In the centre of the rose garden is

a circular pergola with climbing varieties, and in the middle of this arrangement is a small pond and fountain. Elsewhere in Kennedy Park there are raised beds of herbs and fragrant plantings.

Accessible at all times.

Centennial Garden,
Coote Rd, Napier.

The feeling created here is of a huge mountain rock garden. Many very big rocks blend in with foliage plantings. Small shrubs, flaxes and grasses drape over the edges. A high waterfall tumbles into a pond which overflows into another pool. A large bridge can be crossed for another view of the garden. Planted throughout for colour are perennials, bulbs and annuals.

Marine Parade, Coote Rd, Napier.

After the 1931 earthquake the foreshore was the handiest place to dump the enormous amount of rubble created, and it was on this that the garden grew. Napier is fortunate that its 1930s architecture is complemented by gardens of the same period. Visitors can walk from the Centennial Garden down to Marine Parade quite easily. The seafront Parade is an avenue lined with mature trees, mainly large palms and Norfolk pines. Smaller trees and shrubs, beds of perennials and mass displays of annuals are planted nearby. A floral clock , sunken garden and fountain feature.

Accessible at all times. Toilet.

Biddy and Cliff Hair,
"Arcady", 18 Grey Street, Bay View, Napier.   Tel: (06) 836 6661

A large, level, urban garden that features a wide variety of plants. Biddy has imported seeds of perennials, bulbs, shrubs and houseplants. Walk through shade houses, enclosed shelters and heated houses, protecting a host of unusual species, including many types of orchids. Collections of rock and alpine plants, miniature bulbs, roses in flower beds and over archways and lots of climbers, along with a number of potted plantings, add to this colourful and interesting garden. There are unusual plants for sale. The name Arcady means 'a collector's garden'.

Picnics welcome. Teas and lunches for groups by arrangement. Toilet. Visits by appointment from September to March.

Tom and Dora Hartree,
"Te Motu", R.D.6, Puketapu.   Tel:(06) 839 5856

This peaceful country garden has many interesting alcoves. Grass walkways join each place of special interest and there are charming views at each corner. Plantings consist of many different varieties of trees and shrubs, and choice collections of rhododendrons, azaleas, camellias, magnolias and conifers. These are mostly underplanted with perennials, bulbs and ground covers. Irises are a favourite and there is a wide selection, including some which favour damp, boggy conditions. Roses appear throughout other herbaceous beds. The Hartrees are tree people and their home garden has enveloped large areas of the farm where special selections of trees have been planted. Ponds and a natural lake are home to many waterfowl.

Visits by appointment. Donation to Cransford Hospice.

Pam and Brett Train,
"Te Puni", R.D.6, Puketapu.   **Tel:(06) 839 5864**
A hilltop garden, Te Puni has a magnificent view over the countryside towards the
Kaweka Ranges and the gently sloping lawn in front of the house has a haha so as not
to spoil this treat. Plantings in the Trains compact country garden are in corners and
alcoves. Paved steps and paths connect throughout. Archways, pergolas, a number of
seats and a collection of figurines add interest. Lots of flowering shrubs, including
camellias, blend with natives, conifers, beds of perennials, bulbs and roses. Climbers
and ground covers are a feature.
Visits by appointment.

Doris and Owen Birchall,
2 Ngarimu Cres, Taradale, Napier.   **Tel:(06) 844 2550**
This urban corner garden has a stream on one side providing a cool area where ferns
and foliage plants thrive. Other plantings are mixed trees and shrubs, also mass displays of perennials, bulbs and annuals. Choice conifers, unusual deciduous trees,
many Proteaceae and roses give this pretty garden year-round interest.
Visits by appointment.

John and Gaynor Carswell,
"Waipuna", R.D.4, Napier.   **Tel:(06) 839 8805**
Rhododendrons are the main shrub in this split-level country garden. Conifers, roses,
a small rock garden and a variety of bulbs and perennials add spring colour.
Visits mid October to mid December by appointment.

Patsy and Ron Hartree,
"Mahoe", R.D.4, Napier.   **Tel:(06) 839 8852**
Mahoe features many varieties of trees and shrubs growing on 40 hectares. There are
rhododendrons, maples, cherries, tulip trees, natives, conifers, walnuts and many others. Spring is probably the best time for visiting, as the blossom trees, daffodils and
bluebells provide a mass display of colour. Summer shows the leaves and the
cardiocrinums which are scattered through large areas to advantage. Autumn also has
its glory with the turning leaves of the many deciduous trees. Dams are dotted throughout Mahoe, accounting for its prolific birdlife.
Visits by appointment.

John and Star Absolom,
"Rissington", R.D. 4, Napier   **Tel:(06) 839 5836/Fax(06) 839 5859**
Tall, stately Mediterranean cypresses form an avenue along the driveway and generally
dominate the scene in this level, mixed-planted country garden. A large pond edged
with damp-loving species, masses of agapanthus, both old and modern roses, camellias, rhododendrons, natives, lots of deciduous and blossom trees form the main plantings and beds have perennials, bulbs and ground covers. A pink tea rambler frames the
front of the house and is a picture in spring. An extended look is achieved by tree
plantings in the surrounding paddocks.
Visits by appointment.

Pat Gordon,
"Wharehau", R.D.4, Napier.   **Tel:(06) 839 8873**
This large rambling garden is developed on a hillside, with grass walkways and lawn patches on various levels. Plantings consist of rhododendrons, camellias, azaleas and magnolias, some of which are underplanted with perennials, bulbs and ground covers. A woodland garden beneath canopy trees features a huge Wellingtonia redwood (around 80 years old). A newly developed laburnum walk, a rock garden with small ponds, and a waterwheel make a delightful entrance.
Visits by appointment.

Penny and Randall Simcox,
"Braehead", Puketitiri, R.D.4, Napier.   **Tel:(06) 839 8870**
A garden situated on a sloping section under the Kaweka Ranges 500 m above sealevel. Plantings consist of rhododendrons, camellias, roses, flowering shrubs, bulbs, perennials and creepers, among rock gardens and meandering paths. Below the main garden is a dam planted with hostas, astilbes, primulas, *Cardiocrinum giganteum*, irises and other water-loving plants. Best in spring and early summer.
Visits by appointment. Entry fee. There is also a nursery selling hardy shrubs, trees and perennials, and a recently restored 100-year-old whare, 'The Matchbox', with gifts and local crafts for sale.

Rob and Eileen Whittle,
"Little Bush", Puketitiri
Postal address: Private Bag 6404, Napier.   **Tel:(06) 839 8605**
A large woodland garden developed alongside a stand of native bush where birds are fed all year. There is a collection of rhododendrons (some of which have been grown from seed), azaleas and camellias and, to add to the spring colour, there are thousands of daffodils, irises and lilies. A grove of birch trees contains 13 varieties. The long, winding driveway should be walked if possible. Best time October and November.
Please phone in the evening for visits by appointment. Morning and afternoon teas are available at a small fee for groups by prior arrangement. Entry fee $3.00.

Joanna and Angus Hyslop,
"Thurlsholm", P.O. Box 153, Hastings.   **Tel:(06) 874 3721**
Thurlsholm is a large country garden with delightful views of the Hawke's Bay country side. A number of well-established trees line the drive and surround the house. Flower beds are mass planted in perennials, bulbs, a selection of old fashioned and modern roses; and rambling roses, wisteria, clematis and the potato vine cover a long pergola. Another feature is a semi-circle surrounded by more rambling and bush roses blending with perennials and self-seeding annuals; all colour coordinated. Lots of white is predominant throughout. A new developing area is an avenue of *Acer saccharinum* with wild meadow flowers and a seat at one end for resting and enjoying the rural views. A large collection of potted geraniums is a favourite feature. An all-year garden.
Visits by appointment. Entry fee. Accommodation for 7 people. Joanna is an agent for M'Lady Fashions.

Cornwall Park,
Tomoana Rd and Roberts St, Hastings.

Cornwall Park is a large area with a lake and a waterway over which are several bridges. Small islands are home to waterfowl. Features are an enclosed tiled and formally laid out rose garden, a large group of magnolias and a collection of natives. Throughout the park are tall conifers and deciduous trees, with beds of perennials and mass displays of annuals. A hothouse, open from 10 a.m. to 4 p.m. daily, is planted out in tender potted plants and flowers.

The park is accessible daily.

Denis and Florence Brownrigg,
"Mustang Park", Douglas Road, Poukawa, Hastings.   Tel:(06) 874 8801

Florence's garden is around 10 years old. Developed on a large gentle slope, the extensive lawns are edged with scalloped flower beds and some central feature ones. Plantings throughout are of mixed varieties of trees, shrubs, perennials, roses, bulbs and ground covers. Ornaments, archways, a bird loft, steps and a small pond add interest, there are also potted plants and lovely rural views all around.

Visits all year by appointment. No Sunday visitors. Entry fee.

Robin and Doug Nowell-Usticke,
"Wahi Pai ", P O Box 372, Hastings.   **Tel:(06) 874 2863/Fax: (06) 874 2888**
A large country garden on different levels and with easy walking. Plantings are mixed, with a favourite being old-fashioned roses, both bush and climbing varieties. Many of these ramble over the front of the house and around a tennis court. A small intimate gravel courtyard, woodland area and clipped hedging are features, with many of the beds being colour coordinated.
Teas and luncheons by arrangement. Accommodation for 7 people. Visits by appointment. Entry fee.

Diane and Peter Arthur,
"Waikonini", Fernhill, Hastings.
Postal address P.O. Box 610, Hastings.   **Tel:(06) 874 2872**
This large country garden offers great variety. The area around the house is full of Diane's favourite plants: old roses, perennials, shrubs, alpines and natives. Peter cares for the larger varieties, such as rhododendrons, camellias, magnolias, and the cool-loving plants under these. A new addition has been a joint effort: it includes roses, roses and more roses! A tour of this garden starts with a long walk through a pergola, across a log bridge and past a gravity-fed fountain, and then into an area which is surrounded by 50-year-old Lombardy poplars and upright cherry trees. In spring, there is a mass of daffodils. The walk finishes at a 'rosebo', a circular dome covered with old roses. As both Diane and Peter are plant people, they have established many hundreds of trees around their farm, including blossom, nut, coniferous and deciduous varieties.
This garden is open from the Saturday morning of the second to last weekend in November till nighfall on the Sunday of the last weekend in November: times 9 a.m. till dark. Picnickers welcome. Touchwood Books, also here, will be open for business during these times.

Ruthven and Linora Buchanan,
"Lockwood", P.O. Box 1253, Hastings.   **Tel:(06) 874 2867**
In spring and summer this dry, hillside, north-facing garden is a pretty sight, despite all the wind it catches. Developed in terraces and with paths throughout, the plantings feature mixed trees and shrubs, with mass displays of perennials, bulbs, ground covers and roses, both modern and old-fashioned. Linora grows seeds of unusual varieties and describes herself as a collector of plants.
Visits by appointment.

Prue and Jamie Lowry,
"Oreka", Fernhill, Hastings.   **Tel:(06) 874 3871**
A restful country garden is being established here with native trees and shrubs complemented by new plantings. A gully at the bottom of a sloping lawn is filled with perennials, bulbs and roses. Prue is fond of plants which seed themselves and make a mass effect. A semi-circular pergola at the front of the house has various climbers, such as wisteria, roses and clematis, and this makes a delightful feature at the entrance.
Visits by appointment.

John and Phillida Russell,
"Tuna Nui", R.D.9, Hastings.   **Tel:(06) 874 3702**
This is an old garden and its main feature is the setting of mature trees. It is an informal
garden with no particular emphasis on any one species. The owners aim is to maintain
an attractive and reasonably interesting garden for the use and enjoyment of their family and friends. Tuna Nui is particularly appealing in spring and autumn.
Visits by appointment.

Dorothy and Robin Bell,
"Tradgard", Pukehamoamoa,
R.D.9, Hastings   **Tel: (06) 874 3708**
Development of this large informal and relaxing country park garden began at the end
of 1992. Gently sloping and level walking features include a pond with ducks, archways, pergolas, a bridge, raised beds using rocks and posts, and a comprehensive
collection of trees in groups and as specimens. All these give the garden its Swedish
name Tradgard (meaning tree garden). Flowerbeds are a mixture of many roses and
perennials. A colourful sight over spring, summer and with good autumn leaf display.
Open Labour weekend to end of March, Thursday to Sunday, and visits by
appointment Monday to Wednesday 10 a.m. to 5 p.m. Entry fee $5 (honesty box).
Picnics welcome. Suitable for wheelchairs. Toilet. Children's playground is a future
development. Situated 2 minutes from Napier and Hastings. Dorothy is a quilter and
has her handiwork on view.

Rew and Stephen Kyle,
"Tiree Fuchsias", 18 Tomoana Rd, Hastings.   **Tel:(06) 878 4411**
Fuchsias are planted in the garden as well as in a large display shelterhouse. Stand-
ards, hanging baskets and bush varieties. Very pretty from Labour Weekend to the end
of February. Plants can be purchased during this time.
Open Thursday, Friday and Saturday.

Helen Whittaker,
"Wharehuna", 1208 Pakowhai Rd, Hastings.
Postal address: P.O. Box 2028, Hastings.   **Tel:(06) 878 3762**
On a large flat area, this private garden has been created from well-established trees
and shrubs and newer plantings of rhododendrons, camellias, azaleas, conifers, and
other deciduous trees such as viburnums and maples. In a newly developed woodland
area, many foliage plants thrive. A small pond is surrounded at one end with damp-
loving plants such as hostas and astilbes. Near the house is a walled garden with long
beds of herbaceous plants and a dovecote. The semi-formal area has a shallow pool
edged with colour coordinated beds of modern roses. Alongside is another group planting
of old roses. A newly planted deciduous azalea garden and an extension of the paddocks into a spring bulbs and large trees development further extend this garden.
Garden visits by prior arrangement only. Toilets available. Adjacent to the garden
is a nursery which is open daily 9 a.m. to 5 p.m. A great number of the plants sold
here can be seen in the garden.

Frimley Park, Frimley Rd, Hastings.
Mature trees of mixed varieties accent the expansive lawns in Frimley Park. The main feature, however, is the rose gardens. Long beds border each side of a roadway, which leads to a circular and formally laid out rose garden. Some beds are of mixed colours, others single. It is a magnificent sight and the perfume is delightful.
Accessible daily.

John and Margaret Renton,
"Glenmore Station", R.D.1, Hastings.   **Tel:(06) 874 9853**
Glenmore Station's spacious garden is set on a hillside. There are gently sloping lawns and the views are magnificent for miles around. The plantings are mainly trees and shrubs with a big variety of conifers, blossom and deciduous trees. Most are planted as specimens. The flower beds are borders and contain perennials.
Visits by appointment.

John Purdie,
"Nenthorne", R.D.2, Hastings.   **Tel:(06) 878 6441**
An interesting garden with easy walks and a touch of formality in the design. Mixed trees and shrubs, magnolias, maples, dogwoods, some camellias and rhododendrons give a cool woodland feeling. This is a distinctive leaf and foliage garden, although there are some old-fashioned roses and modern standards, along with begonias and spring bulbs which add interest and colour. This restful garden is home to many birds.
Visits by appointment.

Louise Moorhead,
"Claremont", Ada St, Hastings   **Tel:(06) 877 8593**
Claremont welcomes the spring with the flowering of a choice collection of rhododendrons underplanted with winter roses and trilliums. Flower beds are group-planted with old-world cottage plants and old roses. Louise likes her garden to wander so there is always something around the corner. A feature brick courtyard is surrounded by rambling roses.
Interested groups are welcome to visit the garden Wednesdays and Sundays mid September till late December. Other times by appointment.

Mike and Sandra Rolls,
"Sequoia Nursery", S.H. 2, Mangateretere, Hastings.
Postal address: P.O. Box 96, Whakatu.   **Tel: (06) 876 6774**
This nursery features a garden with raised beds so the display of the many perennials can be viewed easily. A small water flow becomes a pond. Sandra describes it as a working garden, so all the plants seen can be purchased from the nursery.
Open daily; 8.a.m. to 5 p.m. weekdays and 9.a.m. to 5 p.m. weekends

Duart House, Duart Rd, Havelock North.
Duart House has a large garden and lawn. The wild woodland area nearby has a native bush walk and a pond. The flat areas around the house have an assortment of flower beds, mainly perennials and bulbs mixed with roses. Roses cover pergolas, and other features include some very tall palms and large oak trees.
Accessible daily.

Peter and Maree Forde-Harris,
"Larsbrook", 17 Renolds Rd, Havelock North   **Tel:(06) 877 8661**
Even though this fully planted urban split-level garden endures extremes of heat and cold, there is a wide variety of plants to be seen. Colour plays an important part, as do the flowers, planted for Maree's floral work. Masses of tulips, daffodils, dahlias and annuals grown from overseas seeds fill flower beds, and along with modern and old-fashioned roses, perennials, ground covers, trees and shrubs can be seen. A shade garden, rockery, ponds and waterfall, where large local rocks have been used in construction, is a cool, interesting area. Paths wind throughout the garden. Urns, hanging baskets, pots and tubs with lots of colourful draping plants add contrast. A pretty garden spring to autumn.
  Visits by appointment. Teas by arrangement. Entry fee. Plants for sale.

Dene Thomas,
"Denes Garden Way", St Hill Lane, Havelock North.
Postal address: P.O. Box 19, Havelock North   **Tel:(06) 877 7162**
Denes Garden Way is a comprehensive nursery and display garden, intensively planted and divided into delightful sections and corners. There is so much to see here; plants, pots, urns and statues. There are tables and chairs tor outdoor and garden use.
  Open Monday to Saturday, 9 a.m. to 5 p.m. Groups welcome by prior arrangement; a full tour can be provided.

Keirunga Gardens, Pullet Rd, Havelock North.
The garden slopes away on all sides from this historic house on top of a hill. A feature here is three very big pepper trees. The flower beds are intensively planted with perennials and there are dense plantings of agapanthus covering a steep slope. Gravel paths feature throughout. Rose beds and a flat lawn area front the house, bordered by a mixture of trees.
  Accessible daily. Toilets available.

James and Sally Williams,
"Longacre", R.D.12, Havelock North.
Wonderful views are enjoyed here at Longacre, from Te Mata Peak across the Tukituki River and the surrounding farm land. A haha at the end of a gently sloping expansive lawn lets the farm paddocks and animals become one with the garden. Likewise, another view below, towards a large lake which has skilful tree plantings surrounding it, is quite something. Large trees of mixed varieties have been planted in groups, specimens and for shelter. A shrubbery of rhododendrons, camellias, blossoms and conifers has a walkway through and flower beds are full of spring bulbs and perennials. Climbers, roses, a walled vegetable garden and citrus orchard, and a damp, cool, predominantly foliage garden are interesting features. Spring brings wonderful colour, while autumn has brilliant leaf changes. The garden is home to many birds and the lake to waterfowl.
  Visits for 20 people or more spring and summer only and by written appointment please. Entry fee.

Richard and Angela Wareing,
759 Maraetotara Road, R.D. 12, Havelock North.   **Tel:(06) 874 7834**
Nestled at the foot of high cliffs and between ridges Richard and Angela's garden almost has its own microclimate; what used to be a bare sloping paddock surrounding a disused roadman's cottage has been transformed into a fully planted, very colourful cottage garden. Old-fashioned perennials, bulbs, roses and self-seeding annuals blend with well-designed vegetable patches, picking gardens and a variety of fruiting trees and vines. The ultimate aim is to have a very large area with a wide variety of fruiting species. A natural stream flows through the section enabling bog and wet-loving plants to thrive. A considerable amount of construction work allows for easy walking, with pet and family activities possible. Lots of native birds frequent the garden.
Picnic lunches welcome. Toilet. Visits by appointment.

G. and J. Curtis,
"Birchwood", St Andrews Rd, Havelock North.   **Tel:(06) 877 6492**
Mainly a tree and shrub garden, Birchwood has specimen trees set in sweeping lawns. Choice collections of rhododendrons, dogwoods, conifers and magnolias are among the unusual and special plantings here.
Visits by appointment.

Alice Thrum and Gillian Blackmore,   **Tel: (06) 877 6051**
"Peak Perennials", 23 Toop St, Havelock North.   **Fax: (06) 877 6067**
A perennial garden developed on a hillside. Examples of the potted plants, which can be purchased, are growing in the garden and there are many rare and unusual plants, including some natives. Many plants, including new releases, are imported from all over the world.
Nursery open Thursdays and Fridays, 9 a.m. to 5 p.m. Other times by appointment. Mail order catalogue available.

Leah and Gordon Kelt,
"Roley", P.O. Box 27, Havelock North.   **Tel:(06) 877 7474**
A spacious semi-formal garden developed on a hill top, with different levels and much construction work on banks, walls and steps. Leah describes it as a flower garden, as she can always pick something. A feature is a knot garden set in a courtyard and planted only in green and white. Other plantings are mixtures of trees, shrubs, roses and herbaceous plants.
Visits by appointment.

Clyde Potter,
"Weleda Herb Gardens", Peak Rd, Havelock North.   **Tel:(06) 877 7394**
Postal address: Weleda N.Z. Ltd, P.O. Box 132, Havelock North.
An attractively laid out and comprehensive collection of herbs can be found in this garden. About 200 plants are grown, all for use in the production of medicinal and cosmetic products. There are other plants to enhance and add interest to the garden, which is cultivated using biodynamic methods.
A guided tour is available by prior arrangement. Entry fee. Cosmetics and medicines can be purchased from the dispensary 8.30 a.m. to 4.30 p.m.

Mr and Mrs A. F. Toogood,
"Reviresco", P.O. Box 88, Havelock North.   **Tel:(06) 877 8373**
A gentle, sloping rural garden has been developed in a semi-formal design. Many large deciduous and blossom trees throughout the whole garden create a cool feeling. The emphasis is on old-fashioned roses and companion plants. Clematis feature in the garden, and plantings for perfume are preferred.
   Visits by prior arrangement, during spring and summer only.

Don and Mary Stewart,
Durham Drive, Havelock North.   **Tel:(06)877 7744**
This rural split-level garden includes some semi-formal areas, with mixed plantings of trees and shrubs. Flower beds consist of perennials, bulbs and old-fashioned roses. Archways and pergolas support roses, clematis and wisteria, and there are many steps, banks and walls. The views towards the sea and inland are spectacular, as the garden is perched on top of a high ridge.
   Visits by appointment. Morning and afternoon teas by arrangement. Toilets available.

Peter and Elizabeth Ormond,
"Ormonds Garden and Nursery",
Private Bag, Havelock North.   **Tel:(06) 874 7820**
Ormonds Garden is designed for dry conditions with a happy mixture of natives and exotics, trees, shrubs and flowers. Walkways offer lovely glimpses round each corner and there are superb views of the Tukituki River, Te Mata Peak and the surrounding valley. Plants available in the nursery can be seen growing in Peter's garden. There are extensions going on as it develops further.
   Open 1 September to 30 March, Wednesday to Sunday, 9 a.m. to 5 p.m.; April to the end of August, every Friday to Sunday, 9 a.m. to 5 p.m. Open all public holidays except Christmas and Boxing Day. Other times by appointment.

Shirley Limbrick,
"Awatea", P.O. Box 30, Tikokino.   **Tel:(06) 856 5879**
This level country garden is surrounded by mixed plantings of rhododendrons, camellias, azaleas, some blossom trees and others. Flower beds frame the lawn areas and these are densely planted with perennials, bulbs and companion plants. Shirley is fond of lilies and has a collection of varying types. Climbing roses also feature in this spring and summer garden.
   Visits by appointment.

Peter and Juliet Holden,
"Forest Gate", Ongaonga.   **Tel:(06) 856 6825**
Here, a formal country garden surrounds an historic house. Brick walls and steps are featured. A long block wall supports some rambling roses and a haha enhances a magnificent view towards the Ruahine Ranges. Flower beds, which edge the sloping lawns, are planted with mixed cottage plants. A very peaceful garden.
   Visits by appointment.

Doug and Sue Pacey,
"D&S Nursery", Bridge St, P.O. Box 21, Ongaonga.   **Tel:(06) 856 6858**
From the middle of November to the middle of December there is a colour and fragrance explosion in the Paceys' garden and roses galore, in beds, on fences, archways and pergolas. Old-fashioned bush roses and climbers, David Austin English roses and modern bush roses feature, along with miniatures and climbers.
Garden open all summer and orders can be taken throughout the year. Mail order catalogue available.

Hugh and Adrienne Williams,
"Te Maire", R.D.4, Waipawa.   **Tel:(06) 856 5705**
A two-generation garden has been developed on this large site. The older area has a choice collection of azalea mollis, camellias, rhododendrons, deciduous trees and natives. The new area, developed on a northfacing hillside with wide grass walkways and planted areas, places the emphasis on the protea family and ericas. There is colour and interest all year.
Visits by appointment. Entry fee. Morning and afternoon teas can be provided by prior arrangement. Toilets available.

Donald and Judy Macdonald,
"Mangatarata Station", Waipukarau.   **Tel: (06) 858 8275**
Situated on a rise, this large country garden, designed by Allan Tichner, complements the 100-year-old homestead. From the driveway of woodland plantings to the section, it has panoramic rural views. Extensive lawns edge a lake which is home to white swans and a variety of ducks. Mature trees give shelter and form for the new acres and easy walkways thread amongst them in this garden for all seasons. Mangatarata Station was the second station to be established in Hawke's Bay; the sheds are older than the homestead and make an interesting walk. The garden is at its best in spring although Allan Tichner's good design makes sure the views and the homestead can be appreciated all year.
Visits by appointment. Entry fee. Toilet. Morning and afternoon teas by prior arrangement.

Betsy and Gordon Mackie,
"Misty Flats", Hatuma Rd, R.D.1, Waipukurau.   **Tel:(06) 858 9714**
A country garden with mixed plantings of trees, shrubs, beds of perennials, bulbs, ground covers, herbs and a vege garden. Rustic garden furniture, pergolas and archways are features. Lots of tree plantings surrounding the garden give an extended atmosphere. Modern and old roses, gently sloping lawns and a lovely rural outlook are other added attractions. Betsy has started the interesting art of topiary container plantings.
Garden open every day during November. Other times by appointment. Group bookings to view garden. Entry fee $3. Devonshire teas by arrangement for groups.

Helen and Paddy Morrah,
"Wharekoa", R.D.4, Waipukurau.   **Tel:(06) 855 4743**
The driveway to this pretty garden is through a long tree-lined entrance which has a lovely rural outlook. With an acre of mixed tree and shrub plantings, special attention has also been given to old roses, both climbing and bush varieties, perennials and bulbs. Visitors will find something of interest year-round.
Visits by appointment.

Christabel and Richard Tylee,
"Waikakahi", Nghape Road, Flemington, Waipukurau.   **Tel: (06) 855 4888**
Many trees surround a large rambling country garden and along one side they have created a woodland area where many ground covers have become naturalised. A tennis court, level front lawn, swimming pool area and a sloping front lawn have beds of mixed perennials, roses and shrubs, including camellias. Lots of climbers are attached on all sides of the house. The trees include deciduous trees, conifers, natives and some fruiting varieties. Christabel has a rose-covered cottage from which she sells Liberty Lawn of London fabrics and some interesting creations from this delightful cloth. There is also a sample mail order offered.
Visits by appointment all year.

Brigid and John Ormond,
"Wallingford Station", R.D.4, Waipukurau.   **Tel:(06) 855 4701**
Surrounding this historic house is a large established garden. Some of the oak trees are around 140 years old. There are sweeping lawns and formal gardens with brick work. At one side, a woodland garden has a rambling path through it. Some flower beds have mixed plantings of perennials, old-world plants and roses, and the best time for colour is spring and summer.
Visits by appointment.

Hamish Kynoch and Julie du Fresne,
"Kynachan", R.D.1, Takapau.   **Tel/Fax:(06) 855 6570**
There is a wide plant variety to be seen in this large easy-walking country garden with rural views. Tall trees provide shelter and dappled light for woodland parts where many shade-loving perennials and ground covers thrive. Mature camellias have been pruned to reveal the trunks and these are also underplanted. Long banks have a host of different draping foliage and flowering ground covers. A cottage area with surrounding flower beds of old-fashioned perennials and masses of bulbs is very colourful over spring and summer. Julie's interest in gardening follows through to her column 'The Good Gardener' in *North & South* magazine. Easy, wide sealed drives enable pleasant viewing even for wheelchairs. Huge deciduous azaleas, magnolias, rhododendrons, natives, potted plants and fantail doves are just some of the features.
Visits by appointment, groups only please.

Larry and Jane White,
"Barnsdale", R.D.1, Takapau.   **Tel:(06) 855 6813**
Developed by late Tom and Pru White, this woodland garden of 12 hectares is basically an arboretum. There are special and rare trees, collections of rhododendrons,

camellias, conifers and old-world roses. Throughout are naturally occurring native trees. Spring brings thousands of English snowdrops followed by bluebells, then the cardiocrinums make mass displays for summer. Autumn has wonderful leaf colouring. The whole area is a haven for native birds.

Visits by appointment. It takes time to see this property. Donations for charity are accepted.

John and Irene White, "Sentry Hill", R.D.1, Takapau.   **Tel:(06) 855 6861**
A rambling woodland garden developed on a hillside with a pond at the bottom. Plantings are mainly trees and shrubs, with a collection of rhododendrons, birch trees, conifers, camellias, and other blossom and deciduous trees. Many of the plantings are grown from seed by John as he is a keen tree person. Grass paths reach all corners and there are many lovely vistas along the way. Both spring and autumn are colourful. Many treasures to be seen here.

Visits by appointment.

Jocelyn Bligh,
"Woodlands", Ashley Clinton, R.D.1, Takapau.   **Tel:(06) 855 6870**
Woodlands is aptly named as it is filled with trees and shrubs, including old rhododendrons, camellias, magnolias, maples and conifers. One notable tree here is a *Davidia* which is about 10 m tall. Lots of bulbs, such as bluebells, daffodils, snowdrops and cardiocrinums have naturalised beneath the canopy. The small flower beds are planted with mixed perennials and bulbs which add colour. Something interesting is to be found in this garden all year round and there is a surprise in every corner.

Visits by appointment.

Mr and Mrs C. Poulton,
"Hillcroft", Rangitoto Rd, Takapau.   **Tel:(06) 855 8231**
Hillcroft is a country garden set on a sloping section. A bank along one side has been developed in terraced gardens with grass paths. Rustic fences and archways support old-fashioned climbing roses, and beds are planted with perennials, bush roses, bulbs and old-world companion plants, many of which have naturalised themselves. The outlook from the front of the house across the plains towards the Ruahine Ranges is quite spectacular. The garden is best in late spring and early summer.

Visits by appointment. Donations to charity welcomed.

Edwyn and Jenny Kight,
"Akitio Station", Private Bag, Dannevirke.   **Tel:(06) 374 3519**
Sweeping lawns feature here, as do large trees. There are also rose beds, perennials and bulb plantings. Development of other areas is an on-going battle against the strong coastal winds which dictate to some extent the varieties which can be planted. Delightful river and sea views.

Visits by appointment.

Norma and Ian Pedersen,
"Glendane", 42 Victoria Ave, Dannevirke.   **Tel:(06) 374 6453**
Glendane is a peaceful garden in a rural area with mixed plantings of maples, rhodo-

dendrons, camellias and other trees. One feature is a large shallow pond with a waterfall and fountain surrounded by stonework and rock garden subjects. Another is a formal area of brick walls, steps and rose gardens. Many intriguing corners with ferns, begonias, perennials and succulents add interest.

Visits by appointment. Entry fee. Handspun and handcrafted woollen garments for sale.

Gwen Fairbrother, "Tangmere", 40 Guy St, Dannevirke.   Tel:(06) 374 7495
This small town garden is a collector's gem, full of camellias and small shrubs underplanted with bulbs, perennials, alpines and some roses. Here you will always find something of colour and interest. Many of the plants have been grown from seed by Gwen herself and she often has potted plants for visitors, as well as a cup of tea.

Visits by appointment.

John and Jill Burn,
"Kowhai Glen", Kiritaki Rd., R.D.2, Dannevirke.   Tel: (06) 374 5452
This country garden was started in 1986. It is terraced in 3 levels; the upper level, which is hot and dry, is planted with suitable shrubs and plants. As the ground is very stony the Burns have made use of these stones by linking different areas with stone retaining walls. On the lower levels, existing totaras, kowhais and other natives have provided a canopy for rhododendrons, camellias, magnolias, maples and hostas, providing a shady tranquil contrast. Primula, iris and ferns line the sides of a meandering creek.

Visits welcome by appointment. No entry fee. Teas available by prior arrangement. Situated 1st house on right of Kiritaki Road which is off Main Highway South before the Oringi Bridge.

Susan and Tony Dalby,
"Roydon", R.D.1, Mangaorapa,
Te Uri Rd, Porangahau.   Tel:(06) 855 5060
This large country garden, set on different levels, has been developed in areas to create views at every corner. The beds are closely planted with various perennials, bulbs and old-world plants, including many special varieties of old roses. Each area is colour coordinated. Rose-covered pergolas and archways join the areas together. Plantings of camellias and large trees create cool places and there are grass walkways throughout. A very pretty garden in spring and summer.

Visits by appointment. Donations are accepted for Save the Children Fund.

Ted and Celia Snelling,
"Peachhaven", 49 Grey Street, Woodville.   Tel: (06) 376 5763
This garden was developed around 1977 to complement the then new home. A large eucalyptus gum dominates the front boundary while a large variegated liriodendron and a pink flowering chestnut shelter other trees and shrubs in the back borders. Extensive lawns show off shrub borders; a strong feature is a comprehensive collection of miniature and bush roses. A restful area with a 3-tier waterfall set amongst shrubs and provides an ideal setting for teas.

Visits by appointment.

James and Bev Armistead,
"Awapai", Bluff Rd, R.D.1, Woodville.   **Tel/Fax (06) 376 4533**
A level country garden which is still being developed. Major focus in the spring is the extensive planting of over 350 roses. Bulbs, shrubs, annuals and overhead trees add the contrast. A gazebo, pergola, pool and playhouse are interesting extras. Wheelchair access, picnic facilities, toilet.

Visits by appointment only during summer months. . Entry fee $2. Teas available by prior notice. Ample parking. Situated 10 minutes from Woodville, 40 minutes from Palmerston North.

Wairarapa

R. Abraham,
"Borderlands", R.D.3, Pahiatua. Tel:(06) 376 7071

A large rambling country garden with a naturally flowing stream, Borderlands is only 20 minutes from Palmerston North. Colour and interest all year comes from a collection of choice trees and shrubs, rhododendrons, camellias and maples. The beds are underplanted with many varieties of bulbs and perennials, and wisterias, clematis, rose and lilies feature throughout. Plant sales.

Ample parking for cars and coaches. Picnic tables available. Open Saturday, Sunday and public holidays, 10.30 a.m. to 5 p.m. beginning Saturday closest to 1 September and closing after the last weekend in April. From the second weekend in December, please phone for opening times as the garden will not necessarily be open on a regular basis. The above times may vary from year to year. Entry fee. Toilet available.

Peter and Heather Hewitt,
"Balfour Farm", R.D.4, Pahiatua Tel:(06) 376 7496

This is a large, level woodland garden with a natural small stream beside which various bog and shade plants grow. Large English trees shelter numerous camellias, rhododendrons and lots of perennials, ground covers and bulbs which have naturalised. Extensive lawns have beds of more rhododendrons, camellias and perennials with roses around the outsides. Specimen blossom and deciduous trees dot the garden. Clipped box hedges, a vege patch and orchards add interest. A new meadow garden with mown walking paths and lots of camellias, rhododendrons and deciduous trees in the tall grass provide contrast.

Visits by appointment.

Marion and Jack Hunt,
"Twin Oaks", 24 Cambridge St, Pahiatua.   **Tel: (06) 376 7462**
Developed on a gentle slope and a gully with the swift creek Keremutopo flowing
through, there bridges to cross, resting places and tame eels to be seen in a large town
garden. Plantings include lots of perennials, leucadendrons, rhododendrons, roses and
climbers over archways and pergolas. Natives, fuchsias and dahlias thrive under the
spread of two huge oak trees. Sealed and brick walkways and steps wind throughout.
A colourful garden spring and summer.
*Visits by appointment. Donation box for charity. Picnics welcome. Garden available
for wedding ceremonies and photography.*

Sara and Arthur Waugh,
"Surreydale", R.D.2, Pahiatua.   **Tel:(06) 376 6235**
Developed on a hillside, this garden has grass paths throughout. Plantings are mixed,
with rhododendrons, camellias, conifers and blossom trees. Leafy plants, such as hostas and lilies, grow in a damp area. An interesting feature is a viewing platform
overlooking the garden in front of the house, which provides a delightful rural vista.
Visits by appointment.

Alan and Joan Vial,
"Te Taumata", R.D.2, Pahiatua.   **Tel:(06) 376 8462**
This all-year country garden is on both flat and steep sloping land. Joan plants for
colour throughout the seasons. A variety of rhododendrons, camellias and fuchsias are
the main plantings, and these are mixed with perennials, bulbs and roses.
Visits by appointment

Kerry Carman,
"Wylde Green Cottage", P.O. Box 805, Masterton.
A garden that is planted and tended by a writer and artist, it resembles many garden
pictures. Fragrance and winter-flowering plants are important, so that flowers can be
either picked or painted all year. Beds are colour coordinated with lots of treasures
which include bulbs, perennials, ground covers, rock plants, blossom trees, old-fashioned roses, natives, camellias, rhododendrons, hydrangeas, magnolias, daphnes and
many more. A pergola, numerous potted plants, some statues and a bed of mostly
antique plants, called a nosegay garden, add to the interest in this compact, cosy, city
garden. Varieties of annuals are used for constant colour.
*Groups by appointment. Due to heavy workload, please book visits with ample
notice in writing to the above address.*

Tom and Di Bunny,
"Te Roto", R.D.11, Masterton.   **Tel:(06) 372 4800**
Designed around family living, this country garden on a level section is divided into
areas. A sunken, enclosed pond garden has large overhead trees such as oak, acer and
lime underplanted with rhododendrons, camellias and damp-loving perennials — paths
and steps meander throughout. The enclosed family utility part has potted plants,
climbers and a pleasant mixture of trees and shrubs. Deciduous trees, blossom trees,
roses, a massive *Lawsoniana* and a *Wellingtonia* are other features. A colonial cot-

tage named Acorn Cottage with accommodation for 6 people is attached to the garden. It is fully self-contained.
Gardens open most weekends and week days. Entry fee.

Gaye Pointon,
"Country Harvest", Morris Road, Te Oreore, Masterton. Tel:(06) 378 6710
Cottage plants blending with herbs surround this house and shop. A picking garden, which is a blaze of colour during spring, supplies flowers for drying (these can be purchased). Gaye puts together baskets, bouquets and bunches.
Garden open October to Easter, but the shop is open all year.

Debbie and Julie Tutty,
"Fleetwood Gardens and Nursery",
Upper Plain Road, Masterton.   **Tel: (06) 378 8340**
A large level garden with open and enclosed areas connected by archways, gravel and grass paths. Collections of rhododendrons, conifers, camellias and natives blend with beds of mixed perennials, bulbs and ground covers. Lots of annuals make a fine showing all through summer, a raised rock wet garden, numerous fuchsias, succulents anda family area add interest. Stone and posts have been used in construction and

there are seats throughout for visitor enjoyment. A comprehensive nursery features many of the plants seen in the garden.

Open daily December to March, 9.a.m. to 7 p.m.; April to November, 9.a.m. to 5 p.m. Bus groups welcome by arrangment.

Shamus Borthwick,
"Waitui", R.D.10, Masterton.   **Tel:(06) 377 1382**
A glorious view over a lake on two sides and beyond over the rural countryside is one of the delightful aspects of this large country garden. The house is situated on a hill top and the garden falls away on all sides creating a challenge for the owners. Considerable construction work has resulted in terracing and wide walkways, steps and paths offering lovely views throughout. Plantings include rhododendrons, camellias, natives, conifers, roses, a number of Australian shrubs and numerous climbers. A host of species bulbs flowering from spring onwards are some of Robin's specialities. The garden is home to a wide variety of bird life.

Groups only by appointment spring and summer please.

Errol and Mike Warren,
"Rata Hills", R.D.11, Masterton.   **Tel:(06) 372 4834**
A deep gorge alongside a house garden has been terraced, stepped and planted in a variety of trees, shrubs, bulbs and ground covers. Many natives form the overhead canopy for rhododendrons. On the upper level, tall kanuka, kowhai, lancewoods and maire trees shelter more rhododendrons, camellias, cherry trees, many perennials, roses, bulbs and ground covers. A large *Magnolia grandiflora,* which is at least 100 years old, is a dominant feature in front of the house. Errol plants lots of flowers for drying and she uses these to create a number of arrangements that visitors can purchase. Native birds are constant inhabitants in this peaceful garden. A lookout platform is underway so the view down the gorge can be appreciated.

Open September to the beginning of December. At other times by appointment. Entry fee.

Judith Callaghan,
"Dursley", R.D.11, Masterton.   **Tel:(06) 372 4804**
Designed originally by Mr Buxton, this large woodland garden has undergone lots of new restoration. Large trees shelter and create conditions for drifts of colour where bulbs, ground covers and annuals have naturalised. Rhododendrons, camellias, conifers and masses of perennials blend with really old old-fashioned roses, a large weeping silver birch and a striking 70-year-old arbutus tree. Numerous species of lilies, a favourite flower of Judith's, are planted throughout the garden. The design is an important aspect in this garden and from the house the garden flows and is interesting from all angles. The surrounding paddocks have stands of native trees which bring birds to the garden all year.

Open Father's Day (September) to Anzac Day (April) every day. Entry fee. Groups welcome, prior notice appreciated. Toilets.

Bill and Gretchen Dalziell,
"Manawa", Tinui, Masterton.   **Tel:(06) 372 6886**
In this rambling, intensively planted garden, rhododendrons, camellias and magnolias are just a few of the varieties to be seen. Many old-fashioned roses are grown, along with perennials and bulbs. Best viewing times are spring and summer.
Visits by appointment.

John and Bridget Canning,
"Oakbourne Gardens and Nursery",
Annedale Rd, Tinui, Masterton.   **Tel:(06) 372 6641**
Camellias, rhododendrons and blossom trees have been underplanted to create a woodland area in this country cottage garden. Roses (miniature, old-fashioned and modern) are planted throughout and a native section is being developed. The adjoining nursery has plants for sale.
Visits by appointment from September to May. Parking for buses; good shelter for picnics and a swimming pool is available during the summer. Hot water, morning and afternoon teas and lunches by arrangement.

John and Sue Dalziell,
"Grassendale", Tinui, Masterton.   **Tel:(06) 372 6702**
A young garden set on a hill with a bank on the top side and another framing the front. It features walls of local stone, as well as brick, and a small pond surrounded by large beds of perennials, bulbs and herbaceous plants. Camellias, rhododendrons, roses, blossom trees and other deciduous species add form and interest. A bog garden is in the developing stages.
Visits by appointment.

Jill and Bill Maunsell,
"Rahui", Tinui, Masterton   **Tel:(06) 372 6696**
The Maunsells have an all-year garden set out on different levels and areas, each with special names. The homestead garden features old roses, rhododendrons, camellias and companion plants. The hollow is home to many varieties of bog and shade-loving

Garry and Meryn Gibson,
"The Triangle", R.D.9, Masterton   **Tel:(06) 372 6857**
In this garden, developed around family life and activities, the planting emphasis is on roses; bush, climbing and miniatures (mostly modern). These are mixed with perennials, bulbs and companion plants. A very pretty garden in spring and summer, although there is interest year round.
Visits by appointment.

Phyllis and Bill French,
"Beauley", R.D.9, Masterton.   **Tel:(06) 372 6824**
A mixed garden of formal and informal design on different levels, mostly growing modern roses. Large trees surround the garden and the outlook is over interesting taipo ridges. (Taipo is a local Maori term which means 'devil'. The steep jagged rocks have small caves and the wind blowing through them makes a weird sound.)
Open by arrangement or at advertised times. Entry fee. Morning and afternoon teas by arrangement. Toilet available. Crafts such as woollen garments and wood-turned articles may be purchased.

plants. A lookout and water garden feature unusual plants, with an emphasis on many different species of the iris family. The pond is also home to two white swans. Wide grass walkways and winding paths join the areas together. *Open 1 September to 1 May, 7 days. Entry fee. Morning and afternoon teas and light lunches can be supplied by prior arrangement.*

Jim and Airini Pottinger,
Jim and Airini Pottinger,
"Anerley", Tinui Valley, Masterton.   **Tel:(06) 372 6685**
This is not a domestic garden, but a farm which has been planted in trees. There are many varieties to be seen, all of which will grow in harsh coastal conditions. Trees for shelter, shade and conservation are in plantations, valleys, belts and planted as specimens. *Visits by appointment.*

"Alfredton Country Gardens"
For information about the next six gardens contact Ronny Percy or Jan Bendall.

Ronny and Cedric Percy,
"Namoi Gardens", Mangamohoe Rd.,
Off S.H. 52, R.D.2, Masterton.   **Tel: (06) 372 5765**
There are delightful long vistas in this large country garden developed on different levels with many aspects including water features, from some quite small to a large pond which has an island and long hump bridge, lots of huge old totara stumps used as focal points and even supporting climbing roses, and beds of roses and perennials mixed with small shrubs. A considerable collection of trees surround the gardens: natives, conifers and deciduous varieties. While spring is colourful, autumn is just as good. Paths wander throughout and native birds enjoy the garden.
Teas and lunches by arrangement. Entry fee. Visits by appointment. Bed and breakfast accommodation for two. Picnics welcome. Close by is Ihuraua Lake with camping facilities, BBQ, beach, toilet, boating and picnic spots available. For information contact Ronny or Cedric Percy.

Janna and Hugh Blundell,
"Waimea", S.H. 52, Eketahuna.   **Tel: (06) 375 0666**
Developed on a rise with rural views, sweeping lawns and trees beyond the garden create an extended feeling in this large country garden. Janna is fond of white and silver plantings, combining them with many old-fashioned roses, perennials and shrubs. A big collection of natives feature amongst tall deciduous and evergreen trees, and in one area this has formed a woodland garden where underplantings include leafy species, rhododendrons, azaleas and camellias. Railway sleepers and stones have been used extensively for edgings and steps. A small pond at one end of the garden is edged with damp-loving hostas, primulas and assorted varieties.
Entry fee. Visits by appointment. Picnics welcome. Toilet.

Marlene and Donald Robbie,
"Otapawa", Haunui Road, Tiraumea, Eketahuna.   **Tel: (06) 376 7250**
Otapawa is a large relaxing country garden developed on different levels. Tall oak trees are underplanted as a woodland area, a sloping lawn has specimen trees with a bog garden at the lower part, while a hill has zig-zagging paths of brick that lead to a gazebo from which there are lovely views. Many damp bog plants surround a small pond with huge interesting boulders adding character. Beds of perennials and roses feature and an unusual entertaining conservatory shelters hanging baskets, potted plants and is constructed around a tall totara tree.
   Teas and lunches for groups by arrangement. Visits by appointment. Entry fee. Toilet.

Jan and Chris Bendall,
"Wairima", Mangaone Valley Road, Eketahuna.   **Tel: (06) 375 8572**
Trees planted in the 1890s frame this tranquil garden which nestles alongside the Managaone River. A walking path threads through the woodland areas and there are level sweeping lawns. An extended view is through a picket fence to further tall trees in the paddocks beyond. Around the house, swimming pool and tennis court areas contain beds of small shrubs, roses and perennials, a contrast to the big trees. Many natives have been added in recent years and the garden is home to a wide range of native birds.
   Visits by appointment. Entry fee. Teas for groups.

Debbie and Nick Nelson,
"Pah Flat", R.D. 5, Eketahuna.   **Tel: (06) 375 8440**
A large country garden on a level section where the plantings around the house began in the 1920s. The mature trees at the entrance form a woodland area and are underplanted with rhododendrons, natives and lots of plants that have become naturalised; a walkway winds through. More recent long herbaceous borders are planted in perennials and roses. Many daffodils flowering in a paddock alongside the garden are a feature in early spring.
   Visits by appointment.

Sheryl and Peter McKay,
"Moroa", R.D. 3, Eketahuna.   **Tel: (06) 375 8434**
Here is a new country garden, level and with many beds of roses, perennials and small shrubs. A rose pergola leads to a developing woodland area where many rhododendrons and natives appear. A border of yellow cannas on one side and agapanthus with Phoenix palms on the other makes an unusual entrance.
   Visits by appontment. Home accommodation for three.

"Eketahuna Gardens"

The next three gardens can be visited for a day's outing at a small charge. Teas, lunches and accommodation can be arranged. For particulars phone Lynne Sutherland of "Mount Donald". Nearby is the Mount Bruce Wild Life Sanctuary.

Kel and Margaret Lucas,
"Glendon", R.D. 4, S.H. 2, Eketahuna. **Tel: (06) 375 8161**
The house here was built in 1892 and the garden has taken many shapes during the ensuing years. In the 1990s it is still flanked on two sides by mature trees, the sloping lawn has a level upper section and the garden has spread to a wet bog and woodland area. Many natural springs have been turned into small ponds and waterways, each being edged with a variety of relatively wet-loving plants. A grotto area is cool and shady and grows ferns. Many natives, camellias, rhododendrons, perennials, roses and ground covers can be seen. A new meadow garden featuring specimen trees and a larger pond with an island is a recent addition. Margaret will give a talk on the garden and the history of Mr John Cooper, the original owner.
Visits by appointment.

Joy and Bruce Cole,
"Waieka", 71 Stanley St., Eketahuna. **Tel: (06) 375 8136**
Many rooms closely planted are formed by Joy's love of collecting plants in her level town garden. Collections of trees, perennials, bulbs, self-sowing annuals, hedgings and roses mingle together. Archways, ponds, pergolas, fences, bird aviaries, statues and resting seats add to the interest. An apple orchard is also included.
Visits by appointment.

Lynne and Jim Sutherland,
"Mount Donald", Central Mangaone Road, Eketahuna. **Tel: (06) 375 8315**
The Sutherlands are developing a large country garden featuring an extensive lawn, raised rock gardens and flower beds of perennials and roses. A potager is an interesting feature, while the surrounding paddocks have shelter belts planted.
Plants for sale. Dinner, bed and breakfast for four. Visits to garden by appointment.

Sarah Dandy,
"Wainui Wild",
190 Putara Valley,
Eketahuna **Tel: (06) 375 8523**
This rambling garden, developed on the banks of the Mangatainoka River and reaching toward the Tararua Ranges, is full of surprises. Old roses grow well here and in the spring the garden and grounds are alive wtih thousands of daffodils. Garden needs time to enjoy.
Visits by appointment. Plants for sale. Morning and afternoon tea available. Toilet.

Penelope and Tim Bunny,
"Abbotsford Gardens", R.D.9,
Masterton.   **Tel:(06) 378 8763/Fax:(06)378 2829**
Penny's peaceful country garden is at the end of a long tree-lined driveway. It is developed in a series of areas and rooms with firm design lines and planted with a host of perennials, old roses, bulbs and unusual shrubs, many featuring good texture, form and foliage for effect. An archway leads to a cherry walk where a 360° panoramic pastoral view can be enjoyed. Visitors can walk to the paddocks beyond, where many more tree plantings appear.

A nursery incorporated in the garden specialises in the unusual perennials seen and a collection of different hydrangeas. Open Saturdays from September to December and March to May. Other times by appointment. Entry fee.

Denbigh and Vicky Meredith,
"Ngatoka", R.D.9, Masterton.   **Tel:(06) 372 3803**
This garden, on a fairly steep slope, grows a variety of old roses mixed with perennials, bulbs and rhododendrons. A redwood walk is being developed through a plantation beside the house garden. The backdrop is interesting, with the steep taipo ridges (see earlier entry for explanation) framing the garden and house.

Visits by appointment. Entry fee. Morning and afternoon teas can be provided by prior arrangement.

Jane and Aga Terpstra,
"Bennett's Hill Garden & Nursery", R.D.6, Masterton.   **Tel:(06) 377 1948**
A large, rambling woodland garden surrounds this historic house. Sweeping lawns are edged with wide borders of perennials and old roses. Many established trees including oaks and elms, frame the garden area. A large nursery is stocked with a fine collection of perennials and old roses.

Garden open Wednesday and Saturdays, or by appointment for groups. Closed May to end of July.

"Te Ohanga Iris Gardens",
Piki Carroll,
Black Rock Rd, R.D.6, Masterton.   **Tel: (06) 377 3239**
A specialist iris garden featuring bearded, dwarf, intermediate and talls, Spuria, Lousianas, Pacific Coasters, Evansia and Japanese iris species, all in a developing 3-acre garden site. Piki's mother, Frances Love, the well known authority on irises, can be available to give advice to visitors by arrangement with Piki.

Open September onwards. Entry free. Some plant sales. Catalogue available.

The Falloon Family,
"Ditton", R.D.6, Masterton.   **Tel:(06) 372 4882**
Surrounding a house over 100 years old is this large, established, woodland garden. A focal point is a huge English oak, approximately 110 years old. This is mainly an easy-care tree and shrub garden, complemented by perennials and bulbs which have naturalised themselves.

Visits by appointment.

Philippa and Neil Petrie,
"Sulphur Wells", R.D. 11, Masterton.　　　　　　　　**Tel:(06) 372 4815**
Unusual pockets of sulphur springs make this a challenging garden where planting is sometimes difficult. A woodland area with a natural stream is home to rhododendrons. The lawns are large, sweeping and on different levels. Philippa has old roses in all her planted beds, including bush and climbing varieties. Other areas contain mixtures of herbaceous plants, bulbs, flowering shrubs and herbs. There is a rock garden and a courtyard constructed from old bricks.
Visits by appointment.

Queen Elizabeth Park,
Corner of Park Ave and Dixon St, Masterton.
Described by the park director, Mr C. Pugh, as a family park and garden complex, Queen Elizabeth Park has a large collection of conifers, probably some of the earliest planted in New Zealand. A big lake is home to many water birds and nearby is an aviary full of exotic and native birds. An area of formal rose beds adds colour, as does a sunken garden. Annuals, set out in beds, feature in summer. There are also rhododendrons and camellias, as well as blossom trees. The adjacent old cemetery has native trees planted around and through it, giving a woodland setting. A long flat area in High St, set out in formal rose gardens, presents a pretty picture in summer. All these areas are looked after by the Masterton Council Parks Department.
Accessible to the public daily. Toilets available.

Edith and Harry Davidson,
"Arbroath", 33 College St, Masterton.　　　　　　　　**Tel:(06) 378 7174**
Arbroath is a level urban garden where roses predominate; around 250 varieties, including miniatures, large-flowering bush and cluster-flowering bush. Many ornamental trees and shrubs, such as camellias, rhododendrons, azaleas, fuchsias and ericas also feature. There is an aviary full of parakeets, lovebirds and canaries.
Visits by appointment.

Beth and Ross Sutherland,
"Tussie Mussie Garden", 6 Cooper St, Masterton.　　　　**Tel:(06) 377 3473**
A small cottage garden with flowers suitable for tussie mussies, including old roses, herbs and perennials. Features include a native fern glen in a shady area, wooden seats, an arbour, many pots and a pergola. Beth paints and has a selection of her work for sale, as well as some plants.
Garden open to visitors most days but groups by appointment please. Entry fee. Toilet available.

Joan Mutimer,
37 Renall St, Masterton.　　　　　　　　　　　　　　**Tel:(06) 378 6177**
Joan's long, narrow town site has a flow of water through the bottom of the garden. This area is full of special and rare plants and bulbs, as Joan is a collector of unusual specimens. The iris family features, but there are also roses, modern and old-fashioned, mixed with many different perennials and bulbs, making this an especially pretty garden in spring and summer.
Visits by appointment.

Mr and Mrs J. Worley,
"Little Otahome",
R.D.4, Masterton.   **Tel: (06) 377 4140**
The unique character of this beautiful garden, known far and wide, arises from the contrast between the house, set simply in the paddock overlooking a stream, little wood and mountains, and the formal garden across the bridge. Here architectural vistas are framed with trees or hedges, planted exuberantly with colour co-ordinated flowers or foliage, and focussing on low key seats, gates, pots and starling boxes. Double borders planted with roses and long flowering perennials, lead into a garden of grey foliage, yellow and white flowers, and a green foliage border opens into a picking garden.
Visits by appointment.

Bill and Jan Clinton-Baker,
"The Sanctuary", Te Kopi Rd., R.D.4, Masterton.   **Tel: (06) 372 7801**
As the name implies, The Sanctuary is home to a wide range of water birds nesting in the surroundings of a large pond situated below the house site, thus providing delightful views during all seasons. Plantings around the house include beds of perennials, roses and ground covers framing a level lawn, amongst an enclosed paved living area and another enclosed grass area. The bank connecting the lower level to the house side is paved and stepped, featuring many small trees, shrubs, roses, masses of perennials, ground covers, hedges of lavender and catmint, all displaying a brilliant colourful picture. A herb seat, the vegetable garden and lots of climbers around the house walls are other interesting ideas. Amongst some tall trees, a woodland walk is being developed. While being a home for many ducks, there are also free-flying ring neck doves and pigeons and two lovely friendly donkeys.
Visits by appointment November to the end of March. Entry fee. Teas and lunches by arrangment.

Robin and Robin Borthwick,
"Te Whanga", R.D.4, Masterton.   **Tel:(06) 372 7728**
Of interest in this large woodland garden are the many rhododendrons, camellias, azaleas, maples and magnolias. Bluebells, cyclamens, lilies and daffodils have all multiplied and naturalised, forming a carpet of colour. The wide, rambling paths and bridges offer pleasant and easy walking. Around every corner there are delightful vistas and from the house one gets wonderful views of the rural countryside. This is a spring, summer and autumn garden, although winter also has its glories.
Visits by arrangement. It takes time to see this garden properly. Entry fee.

Gordon Knutson, R.D.2, Carterton.
Occupying a large site on different levels, this country garden has a blending of miniature roses, perennials, bulbs, camellias, rhododendrons, and a number of blossom and deciduous trees. A small pond is edged with damp-loving bog plants, and a considerable amount of local stone has been used on banks and steps.
Visits by appointment. Visitors are welcome to lunch on the lawn areas. Toilet.

Mary and Bruce Ross,
"Panorama", Longbush, R.D 4, Masterton.　　　　**Tel: (06) 372 7824**
Panorama is a rambling garden created in different areas. It has a lake and citrus orchard, and there are many unusual and interesting trees and shrubs, as well as roses, perennials and bulbs.
Visits by appointment, small entry fee. Teas and lunches by prior arrangement.

Allan and Jeanette Gates,
"Awaiti", Chester Rd, R.D.1, Carterton.　　　　**Tel:(06) 379 8478**
This large country garden has been developed on a level section with a water aspect. Local stone has been used to form a water race, ponds and falls. Some flower beds are raised, others lowered to add interest. Plantings are mixed, with roses, perennials, bulbs, flowering trees, rhododendrons, camellias and cherry trees. A number of archways support climbing roses, clematis and wisteria. Colour features all year. Goldfish, peacocks, doves and fantail pigeons all to be seen. Well-stocked plant nursery and gift shop selling dried flowers, arrangements and a variety of gifts.
Open 1 September to 31 May. Shop and nursery year round, 10 a.m. to 4 p.m., Tuesday to Sunday (closed Monday). Large groups, prior notice please. Small entry fee to garden. Toilet available. 100-year-old cottage creates an interesting tea room.

Alan and Faye Portman,
"Clareville Nursery", Main Rd, Clareville, Carterton.　　　**Tel:(06) 379 8604**
The emphasis is on perennials in this large country garden designed in a semi-formal pattern. A water race flows through and brick-edged curving beds are mass planted. Old-fashioned roses grow in many areas and over a pergola. Conifers, rhododendrons, camellias, deciduous and blossom trees add height and contrast. A dry garden, that gets neither water nor fertilizer, and a circle planted in pink and silver are features. The nursery has a large collection of perennials and old-fashioned roses for purchase.
Open every day.

Bee and John Blundell,
"Ngaranui", Ponatahi Road, Carterton.　　　　**Tel: (06) 306 9140**
There are old roses everywhere here, blending in beds, over archways, along a long pergola, on fences and along a tennis court surround. Many perennials feature in clump plantings for colour effect including delphiniums, penstemons and lupins. Tall trees at the entrance driveway shelter a woodland area where plantings emphasise foliage. In a gentle sloping lawn there is a small pond with a water trickle becoming a bog garden, ideal for the wet-loving plants. Lots of daffodils are to the fore in the early spring, combining with the early camellias. Posts, battens and stumps have been used for edgings, seats and the rustic rose supports. Lichen-covered local rocks are used for garden framework. A colourful garden spring and summer. Easy walking.
Teas and lunches by arrangement. Entry fee. Visits by appointment. Spare plants for sale.

James and Nola Thompson,
"Cesteria", R.D.1, Matarawa, Carterton.   **Tel:(06) 379 7792**
A large garden with many different areas, including a woodland area, full of larger trees underplanted with rhododendrons, camellias and perennials. Many roses are mixed with bulbs and herbaceous plants in flower beds. A number of blossom trees, lilacs, maples and magnolias start the spring flowering, A small pond is surrounded by bog plants and unusual perennials. Best in spring and summer.
Visits by appointment.

Mrs Jacqui Sutherland,
"Whangaimoana", R.D.2, Featherston.   **Tel:(06) 307 7736**
Landscaped on different levels, Jacqui's large garden surrounds an historic castle-like house. Many trees are dotted round the garden and underplanted with beds of' roses, perennials and herbaceous plants. The emphasis is on spring bulbs and Jacqui has many thousands of them all through her garden, where wide grass walkways and easy steps reveal delightful vistas round every corner. A special feature is daffodil time, 22 August to 6 September. Whangaimoana is at its best from spring to Christmas, but there is interest all year round.
Open every day late August to Christmas, other times by appointment. Entry fee.
Allow plenty of time to view this garden. Morning and afternoon teas and light lunches
can be arranged for groups. 48 kms from Featherston on Cape Palliser Road.

Bill and Elaine Gooding,
"Prairie Holm", Western Lake Rd, R.D.3, Featherston.   **Tel:(06) 308 9090**
Groups of large native trees have been used to their best in the design of this large woodland garden, where plantings of a wide variety of other trees, shrubs, ground covers, bulbs and lots of perennials are in complete harmony. Rhododendrons, camellias, blossom trees and evergreen azaleas blend together to create a blaze of colour throughout spring and summer. Numerous clipped hedgings, local stones, gravel paths and grass walkways define beds. Masses of perennials are underplanted everywhere. A water feature has a fountain, waterwheel and hump bridge over a pond edged with stones that also form rock and alpine beds. Spacious lawns appear in clearings where delightful vistas can be seen.
Open all year, 9 a.m. to 5 p.m. Other times by appointment. Honesty box entry. A
nursery alongside is stocked with a big collection of rhododendrons, azaleas and
perennials. Opening times 1 July to 30 November, 9 a.m. to 5 p.m. Other times by
arrangement. Groups welcome.

Taranaki

Allan and Min Coplestone,
"Mackford Cottage Garden",
Awakino Road, R.D.1, Mokau.   Tel: (06) 752 9760

A country cottage garden with a micro-climate that has wonderful views of the Mokau River and surrounding native bush reserves. The mass plantings extend to the woolshed area which is close by. Min is a weaver and has items for sale.

Visits by appointment. Small entry fee. Home stays for 4 people. Coach groups welcome — bring picnic lunch. Tea, coffee and cold drinks supplied. Trips can also be arranged with the historic creamboat launch trips which come to the cottage for lunch. 9 kms off S.H.3.

Felix, Mark and Abbie Jury,
"Tikorangi", Otaraoa Road,
43 R.D., Waitara.   Tel:(06) 754 6671/(06) 7458577

Felix Jury is known internationally for his extensive work in hybridising and plant breeding and many of his specialities can be seen amongst the rhododendrons, camellias and magnolias in his Waitara garden. Other varieties, such as the vireya rhododendrons, azaleas, conifers, native and deciduous trees, can be seen, along with huge rimu trees, some 110 years old, sheltering a host of bromeliads. Rock gardens form one part of the garden and here there are alpines, cycads, yuccas and many miniature bulbs. Trial grounds feature new plants along with many beautiful lilies. Alongside the garden is the fully stocked nursery of magnolias, camellias, vireya rhododendrons, a wide variety of deciduous trees, hostas and unusual bulbs. The focus is on the Jury hybrids. A mail order is available.

The garden is open from September 1st to mid November. Entry fee $4 refundable on plant purchases over $15. Other times by appointment. Nursery open Monday to Saturday all year. 6 km inland from the Methanex Plant, 20 minutes from New Plymouth.

Shirley and Dallas Murray,
"The Kworree", 12 Pukekohatu Street, Waitara.   Tel:(06) 754 4254
The Kworree garden is a closely planted, all-year town garden situated on an old quarry site, hence the unusual name. Developed on different levels creating rooms, plantings include rhododendrons, camellias, conifers and many perennials. A lower section has a cool feeling where tall natives overhead shelter a variety of foliage plants and a small waterway crossed by a bridge. Railway sleepers, concrete pieces and timber have been used extensively throughout, forming raised beds, steps, edgings and archways, box hedging and potted plants are other features.
Visits by appointment.

George and Bev Moratti,
"Stone Haven Garden", 2 Armstong Avenue, Waitara.   Tel:(06) 754 6164
A colourful garden for all seasons featuring large formal rose gardens, mass planted perennial beds, with old-fashioned roses, a developing bog and water garden. Plantings of camellias, rhododendrons, azaleas, magnolias and maples are included. A thyme lawn on the drive and many potted plants add interest. Easy walking.
Home accommodation available. Visits by appointment.

Brent and Barbara Jury,
"Pukeawa Nursery and Garden", R.D.42, Waitara.   Tel:(06) 754 8684
A large steep bank behind the house as well as a steep bank dropping away from the lawn area was a challenge to these two keen gardeners. Their plantings of many natives mixed with conifers, rock plants and ground covers, as well as bulbs, make this a colourful, all-year garden. Their love of cycads and palms has prompted Brent and Barbara to develop a nursery for these plants and they are now specialists in this field. Many of these strongly structured plants feature along a riverbank walk and a 'climbable' rock garden has a 'folly' lookout with delightful views. Brent has a collection of individually designed wrought iron garden accessories for sale.
Visits by appointment. Entry fee.

David and Noeline Sampson,
"Cedar Lodge", 63 Egmont Road,
Bell Block, R.D.2, New Plymouth.   Tel/fax:(06) 755 0369
Cedar Lodge has one of the largest conifer displays in New Zealand, with over 600 different species set out in a unique garden. Visitors are welcome to wander through and see how these useful shrubs grow and which look best grouped together.
Open 7 days; Monday to Saturday 8 a.m. to 4.30 p.m., Sunday 10 a.m. to 4 p.m. Nursery also available to inspect. There are some 400 varieties to choose from.

"Mangati Dahlias",
Rex Stewart, Ken Schischka,
121 Mangati Road, Bellblock, New Plymouth.   Tel: (06) 755 2330
Situated close enough to the sea so that the waves can be heard, this extensive level garden specialises in colourful dahlias. Although there are a number of other features, the prime time for the dahlia flowers is February to March.
Garden open Thursday to Sunday 10 a.m. to 5 p.m. from January to the end of May. Mail order catalogue available. Suitable for wheelchairs. Picnics welcome. Toilet. $1 entry fee includes cup of tea or coffee.

Gordon and Eunice Phipps,
"Blossom Inn", 10 Worley Road, Lepperton.   Tel:(06) 752 0730
A country garden consisting of conifers, roses, fuchsias, maples, copper beech and various other plantings for colour all year around. A wishing well, wheels, fish pond, picnic table and chairs add interest.
Visitors welcome by appointment. Toilets available. Ample parking on road.

Rex and Marie Ostler,
"Cedar Lake", Manutahi Road, Lepperton.   Tel:(06) 752 0819
A wandering woodland garden set amongst a stand of native bush. There are walks through the bush and a number of large trees are named. A developing lake area adds interest. Rex is fond of liliums and hippeastrum bulbs; other unusual bulbs, marsh plants and perennials can also be seen.
Open 7 days, 9 a.m. to 5 p.m. Large groups, a notice would be appreciated. Picnic table available. Toilets.

Denis and Pauline Lepper,
"Te Puke Awa", Lepperton, R.D.3, New Plymouth.   Tel:(06) 752 0840
This large, level, English-designed garden boasts some trees which are over 100 years old. One is a magnificent chestnut tree in the centre of the garden. Elsewhere, a natural stand of natives attracts birds galore. Archways covered with old roses join the different sections. Pauline has planted lots of new rhododendrons, camellias and azaleas. While bulbs predominate in spring, this garden blooms to the end of summer.
Visits by appointment. Toilet available.

John and Elizabeth McBride,
Richmond Road, R.D.3, New Plymouth.   Tel:(06) 752 0807
Here 0.2 hectares of level to gently sloping lawns enclose a water garden with a white garden nearby. There are 50 flowering cherry trees and many conifers, as well as other trees and shrubs. Further landscaping is in progress.
Available to groups of interested people by prior arrangement.

Alyson and Bill Davies,
383 Devon Street West, New Plymouth.   Tel:(06) 758 8321
A well-established city garden with good examples of how expert pruning can keep trees and shrubs to a required height and width in an urban section. Bill is always nipping unwanted branches off camellias, rhododendrons and conifers. This garden always has colour, although it is at its best in spring and summer.
Visits by appointment.

Doug and Rita Proffit,
"Gro-wel Fuchsia Gardens", 84 Brois Street, New Plymouth.
Here is a garden of mixed plantings, specialising in fuchsias; there are many hundreds and many varieties. Polyanthus and orchids are also grown as a hobby. The best time to see the flush of blooms is from the end of October to the beginning of autumn.
Open every day. Picnic facilities. Visitors are welcome to bring their own lunch, and, for groups, hot water can be supplied if prior notice is given.

John Martin,
"Egmont Roses", Cowling Road, New Plymouth.
Postal address: P.O. Box 3162, New Plymouth.   **Tel:(06) 753 4283**
The nursery at Egmont Roses has been specifically laid out for visitors and has over
500 different varieties, all labelled and well displayed. The main flowering season for
the rose fields is from Christmas until the end of April, although some display beds
commence flowering in November.
*The nursery is open 7 days a week, all day, and the office is open for assistance
and advice during business hours, Monday to Friday, 8 a.m. to 4.30 p.m. A free
catalogue is available.*

Pukekura Park and Brooklands,
Liardet Street, New Plymouth.
Close to the city centre, Pukekura Park is a very beautiful, well-established area with
gardens throughout and many pleasant walks. A large lake in the centre is surrounded
by native trees, ferns both large and small, and many exotic trees and shrubs. Rhododendrons feature extensively during spring. There is a waterfall, fountains, a large
bridge to cross, display houses for tender plants and a fernery. The walk continues
past the lake and emerges into the expansive lawn area of the Brooklands Bowl. Here,
there are some large exotic trees underplanted with spring bulbs.
Accessible at all times. Tea house. Toilets available.

Bruce and Ella Kelland,
20 Hurworth Road, New Plymouth.   **Tel:(06) 753 4016**
Occupying 0.4 hectares of native bush, with a lake and a waterfall outlet, this garden
is home to many native birds. A walk meanders through the garden, then bush and
out in the garden again. There are many resting spots and seats from which to enjoy
the vistas and lake reflections. Rhododendrons, camellias and azaleas border the
bush and are throughout the garden, making a splash of spring colour. A tranquil
garden all year.
Visits by appointment.

"Taranaki Rhododendrons",
Susan and Robert Oliver,
691 Carrington Rd,
R.D.1, New Plymouth.   **Tel: (06) 753 3377/A.H: (06) 758 8005**
Taranaki Rhododendrons is a well established large display garden featuring approxi-
mately 1100 of these beautiful flowering trees. A native backdrop, a circle garden of
Lems Cameo rhododendrons, mature magnolias, camellias, azaleas, maples, beeches
and cherries all blend harmoniously together. Peak flowering is mid August to mid
December with large leafed varieties flowering August to September and the Lems
Cameo during November.
*Open to public 1st April to 30th November, Monday-Saturday 9.30 a.m. - 4.30
p.m. Catalogue available. Admission free. Situated 2 minutes from city boundary on
road to Pukeiti.*

Sally and Paul Masson,
407 Frankly Road, New Plymouth.   **Tel:(06) 753 4358**
The garden here is designed to complement the 115-year-old house. Cottage plants
and old-fashioned roses are to the fore and camellias, blossom trees, rhododendrons,

including the vireya variety, add interest. A delightful intimate corner with a small gazebo covered in roses and a formal enclosed garden are special areas. Best from October and December.

Visits by appointment.

Hurworth House, Carrington Road, New Plymouth.

The backdrop of large native and exotic trees shelter historic Hurworth House. Built in 1855/56, the house is administered by the Historic Places Trust and the cottage garden was started in 1976 by their members. Planting is in keeping with the era of the house. One interesting plant is an old chestnut rose still flowering profusely.

Hurworth House is open Wednesday to Sunday including public holidays, 10 a.m. to 4 p.m. For further information contact the curator on (06) 753 6545.

Bill and Nola Pickering,
534 Carrington Road, New Plymouth.   Tel:(06) 753 9574

Nola's garden is a large all-year country garden with a general mixture of trees, shrubs, perennials and bulbs. Rock gardens feature, along with collections of camellias, conifers, protea species and maples. Roses, both modern and old-fashioned, ensure there is always something for floral art work, a favourite pastime of Nola's. Easy-walking paths and contoured lawns.

Visits by appointment.

Pukeiti Rhododendron Trust,
Carrington Road, New Plymouth.

Situated on the slopes of Mount Taranaki, Pukeiti is a unique garden demonstrating a splendid blend of native bush and exotic trees and shrubs. The emphasis is on rhododendrons, and there are many rare and special plants to be found here, along with a large collection of azaleas. A display house shows off the tropical varieties of rhododendrons. Hostas, astilbes, auratum lilies, cyclamen and hellebores complement the camellias, magnolias, viburnums and other exotic plantings. These gardens are world-renowned. Very easy walking tracks link the various sections of the park.

The gardens are open daily 9 a.m. to 5 p.m. excluding Christmas. Entry fee. Teas and light lunches are available at the Gatehouse Restaurant. For further information telephone (06) 751 1140.

Tupare, Mangorei Road, New Plymouth.

The former home of the late Sir Russell Matthews, this well-known garden of 3.6 hectares was started in 1932. There are many different sections to explore on its winding path: woodland walks, bog gardens, streams, ponds and a large lawn area. Tupare is notable for its large collections of rhododendrons, azaleas and camellias, and there are also many splendid maples and cherry trees, conifers and natives. Colour shows to advantage in spring.

The garden is open from 9 a.m. to 4 p.m. daily except Christmas Day. Entry fee. It is administered by the Queen Elizabeth II National Trust. For further information contact Mr Alastair Duncan (06) 758 6480.

Les Taylor,
"Doune", 48 Saxton Road,R.D. 1, New Plymouth.   Tel:(06)753 4623

Les's large woodland garden grows many rhododendrons, camellias, azaleas, magnolias and maples. A steep gully has walking tracks leading to a lake full of bog-loving plants. Old roses, ground covers, conifers, as well as perennials and bulbs, are in abundance. The best time to view this garden is from September to March. Allow plenty of time here.

Visits by appointment. Entry fee.

Alma and Vic Rydon,
50b Budleigh Street, New Plymouth.   **Tel:(06) 753 4889**
This is a collector's garden with many rare and unusual plants. Alma's love of plants is evident in the house as well, for she has created an indoor-outdoor garden sheltering a variety of tropical and sub-tropical plants. There is something in flower all the time.

Visits by appointment.

Ian and Sheryl Swan,
"Tawa Glen", Mountain Road, R.D.3, New Plymouth.   **Tel:(06) 752 0809**
A garden of several hectares, Tawa Glen has some sloping ground fully planted with almost 400 rhododendrons. A grove of large old tawa trees has been extensively planted to create a woodland atmosphere. An area of newer plantings surrounds the house and a large lake. Here one finds camellias, conifers, ericas and magnolias. Sheryl is fond of old roses and has a collection of them. This is an ever-expanding garden.

Visits by appointment. Groups only, please. Entry fee.

Peg and Howard Haylock,
68 McKeller Street, Oakura.   **Tel:(06) 752 7568**
Small, compact, urban and coastal, this garden has mixed plantings of small trees and shrubs amongst perennials, bulbs and ground covers. Raised beds add interest and give height along one side, where there is a path of stepping stones. All-year colour is important to Peg.

Visits by appointment. Picnic lunches welcome. Toilet.

Allan and Hazel Madgwick,
1 Linda Street, Oakura.   **Tel:(06) 752 7742**
A slightly sloping coastal garden which is small and intensively planted. Colourful all year with perennials, bulbs, annuals, small shrubs and roses. Pots, planters and ornamentals are features. Small collection of plants for sale.

Visits by appointment. Teas by arrangement. Toilet.

Glyn and Gail Church,
"Woodleigh Nursery", 743 South Road, Oakura.   **Tel:(06)752 7597**
Featuring rhododendrons, especially the vireya species, this nursery has delightful garden surroundings. A large paddock is set aside for growing trees and shrubs from geographical regions to see if they can grow to their full potential in this area. A large pond is surrounded by damp- and water-loving plants, while tranquil walks through a woodland area show many rhododendrons growing amongst natives. A lovely view can be enjoyed from the house looking down a hillside of perennials and small shrubs to the pond. Two unusual trees to be seen are a floss silk tree (*Chorisia*) and a Mexican hand tree (*Cheirosteman*).

Open every day except Friday, 8 a.m. to 5 p.m., all year.

Tony Barnes and John Sole,
"Ngamamaku", 781 Main South Road, Oakura.   **Tel:(06) 752 7873**
The sound of flowing water can be heard all through this tranquil country garden set alongside and amongst native bush. Ngamamaku means place of the tree ferns and they abound here, as do the native birds. Numerous rhododendrons, camellias, azaleas, maples, magnolias, perennials, bulbs and ground covers feature throughout. Local stone has been used to form many rock gardens. Paths wind throughout with steps and bridges connecting different areas. Statues enhance a number of interesting corners. Formal rose beds and archways are contrasting features, as is a large aviary. Lovely spring colour, although interesting all year.
Visits by appointment.

Joyce Young,
Wairau Road, Oakura.   **Tel:(06) 752 7414**
A level coastal section full of mixed plantings. Planting for flowers for picking is a special focus, as Joyce enjoys floral art. The winding grass paths are easy walking and a delightful collection of pottery pieces made by Joyce enhance surprise corners. Always a pretty garden.
Visits by appointment

Philippa Holman,
Surrey Hill Road, R.D.4, Oakura.   **Tel:(06) 752 7023**
Masses of cottage plants overflow flower beds in this terraced hillside garden. Of interest are collections of salvia and lavender, some of which Philippa has grown from seed. Colour combinations are also important. Herbs can be seen and there are easy-walking gravel paths. New areas are in developing stages. Plants for sale.
Visits by appointment.

Piet and Riet Van Klink,
82 Oxford Road, Okato.   **Tel:(06) 752 4229**
Natives are the important plantings here, forming two sides of the garden's boundary. There are many types and they are closely planted. A collection of azaleas for spring and a long driveway with a thyme strip thrive by the coast and add contrast,
Visits by appointment. Donations please.

Ian and Merle Clark,
Oxford Road, Okato.   **Tel:(06) 752 4208**
This rambling country garden, set atop a hill, enjoys a glorious view towards Mount Taranaki. Plantings are a mixture of conifers, camellias, rhododendrons and roses.
Visits by appointment.

Helen and Ray Rook,
24 Hickford place, Okato.   **Tel:(06) 752 4006 or 752 4035 (wk)**
The sound of running water from the Kaihihi Stream, a backdrop of native bush, superb views from sea to mountain and lots of native birds are all enjoyed in this urban coastal garden. Roses flower spring and summer and contrast with collections of conifers, camellias and native plantings. A sloping section, it is terraced and easy walking.
Visits by appointment.

Barbara Williams,
"Hikurangi", Newall Road, Okato.   **Tel:(06) 752 4058**
Different levels connected by steps and pathways, established areas and new developing ones make up this large country garden. Plantings are mixed varieties of rhododendrons, camellias, assorted trees and shrubs which blend with beds of perennials.
Large lawns and wide grass walkways are easy walking. A woodland area has huge
tree ferns underplanted with different shade plants. Small ponds and a ponga pergola
add contrast. Development is underway around a large lake, home to many water
birds. There are a number of NZ endangered plants to be seen. Historic woodshed
museum.
Visits by appointment. Ample parking. Toilets. Picnics welcome. Entry fee $4.

Syd and Marje Sharpe,
"Sydmar", Warea Rd, R.D 37, Okato.   **Tel: (06) 752 8050**
A coastal country garden, exposed to all winds but enjoying mountain and sea views.
Developed as a two spectrum garden, Marge's colourful intensely planted area and
Syd's colour co-ordinated more orderly one all blend happily together. Features in-
clude rock and bulb gardens and formal gardens. As a watercolour painter of flowers
it is important for Marge to have a variety to study.
*Open during the Taranaki Rhododendron Festival and the 25th of November and
the 25th February 9. a.m. to dusk. Other times by appointment.*

Ken and Audrey Moratti,
39 Maire Street, Inglewood.   **Tel:(06) 756 7527**
This garden has something flowering all year round. A woodland has large trees sheltering shrubs, ferns, rock pools and rock gardens. Audrey has an extensive collection
of cacti and succulents in a glasshouse. During February and March, begonias and
fuchsias make a beautiful display.
Visits by appointment.

Elaine and Des Schreiber,
17 Kauri Street, Inglewood.   **Tel:(06) 756 8278**
Constant colour and interest all year is Elaine's aim in this large, relaxing urban garden. Grass walkways, lawns and raised flower beds follow the contour of the section.
Camellias, rhododendrons, blossom trees, ground covers and masses of perennials
blend together with collections of roses over pergolas, archways and along fences.
Fuchsias are a special favourite; they are outdoors in beds and under shelter in unusual houses where the collection is quite large. Orchids also feature in another large
shelterhouse. Rockeries add to the overall delightful picture.
Visits by appointment.

Lois and Don Mander,
"Mandervilla", Rimutauteka Road, Inglewood.   **Tel:(06) 756 8546**
There are lovely vistas at every corner of this pleasant, peaceful country woodland
garden which has been developed on different levels. A damp, slightly sunken area is
full of hostas, primulas and other damp- and shade-loving plants. Trees and shrubs
are a mixture of native, blossom and deciduous trees, while large palms add contrast.
Spring brings fuchsias and masses of bulbs to the fore. Rockeries made up of local
stone are a favourite.
Visits by appointment. Entry fee $3. Farmstay dinner, bed and breakfast.

Jennifer and Mac Paterson, Tarata, via Inglewood.   Tel:(06) 756 5884
Originally on a level area, this garden now spreads over different levels, creating an interesting design. Some large silver birch trees shelter a multitude of spring bulbs, and there are many rhododendrons and camellias. Jennifer says her garden is comfortable and lazy. It occupies a tranquil setting next to an 100-year old store.
Visits by appointment.

Kevin and Maureen Bunn,
Mania Poto, R.D.7, lnglewood.   Tel:(06) 756 5536
This garden, after being added to over the years, now covers 0.8 hectares, with tracks joining the different areas. Bridges cross the stream, and cherry trees, rhododendrons, azaleas and camellias, along with natives, are mass planted. It takes time to explore this garden, which is nestled in a pleasant valley.
Visits by appointment. Visitors are welcome to bring lunch, and tea can be provided. Toilet available.

Margaret and Richard Hodges,
Tarata, R.D.7, Inglewood.   Tel:(06) 756 5526
This is a large relaxing country garden with smooth sweeping lawns on different levels. Established trees, rhododendrons and camellias are underplanted with a big collection of perennials, including an interesting range of hostas. A more formal area beside a grass tennis court has traditional wide herbaceous borders. A newly developed farm pond is surrounded with plantings of bog- and water-loving species, including astilbes, irises and primulas.
Visits by appointment. Toilet. Picnics welcome. Homestay for five. Entry fee.

Trevor Simpson,
"Island Holm", Ngaro Road, R.D.10, Inglewood.   Tel:(06) 762 4817
Roses are everywhere in this delightful garden; there are over 2000 plants — climbing, miniature, old-fashioned and modern. Many other trees and shrubs complement the roses and hundreds of spring bulbs make a colourful display from September through to March.
Visits by appointment. Morning and afternoon teas can be provided for groups by prior arrangement.

McCullough Dell, King Edward Park, Stratford.
A large grassed area is surrounded by trees in this dell. In spring, a lake reflects the many flowering cherry trees and there are rhododendrons blended with a variety of conifers, deciduous trees and camellias. This area is a delight to visit during spring. Alongside is a pleasant bush walk which crosses the river several times.
The gates are not open for driving through, but are always open for walking. Picnic tables and seats available. Toilets are to be found at the netball pavilion. The grounds are tended by Parks and Reserve personnel headed by Mr Ron Bray.

Mrs M.I. Devine,
2 Miranda Street, Stratford   Tel:(06) 765 7297
Described by its owner as a woman's garden, this Stratford property has many rhododendrons. Camellias and magnolias complement the layout, as does the bed of roses. Spring bulbs and perennials are underplanted everywhere.
Visits by appointment.

Barry Hughes,
6 Oberon Street, Stratford.   **Tel:(06) 765 7036**
An intensely planted 0.3-hectare urban garden terraced on one side. Unusual shrubs
and plants can be seen, along with rhododendrons, camellias, native and blossom
trees. A plant-person's garden. A damp spring area has relevant plants thriving.
Visits by appointment.

Richard and Eileen Morling,
4 Brecon Road, Stratford.   **Tel:(06) 765 8374**
Springtime is when this garden is best viewed. A hillside is terraced with paths and
plantings include rhododendrons, camellias and cherry trees. Water flows out of a
cave to form a waterway through the lower part of the garden, with the sides planted in
damp-seeking plants.
Visits by appointment.

Frances & Gordon Gray and Alison & Pat Murphy,
14 & 16 Antonio Street, Stratford.   **Tel:(06) 765 6116** or **765 7341**
A section that falls away steeply to a delightful cool woodland garden where a small
stream flows through. Crossing the bridge leads the visitor to plantings of rhododendrons, camellias and natives. The view from the house is especially tranquil. Camellias
and rhododendrons are planted on the top level and a number of roses feature as well.
Visits by appointment.

Noel Petrie,
124 Brecon Road, Stratford.   **Tel:(06) 765 6043**
A lake at the bottom of a gently sloping lawn is the focal feature in this urban garden.
The backdrop here is plantings of rhododendrons, azaleas, conifers, natives and tree
ferns. Both sides of the section have long lines of camellias and rhododendrons. In a
shelterhouse, orchids and tuberous begonias thrive. Best in spring.
Visits by appointment.

"Ngaere Gardens"
Shirley and Clary Hart, Mountain Road,
R.D. 23, Stratford.   **Tel: (06) 765 6614**
Ngaere Gardens is 10 acres of mature trees, lakes, fountains and gardens. The historic
lakes were formed in the late 1800s and resemble in shape the North, South and
Stewart Islands — probably the only place in New Zealand where you can find New
Zealand situated approximately 8km south of Stratford!
Open 7 days. Light lunches available on request. Entry fee.

Shirley and Ian Greenhill,
1a Hamlet Street, Stratford.   **Tel:(06) 765 7338**
Many camellias, rhododendrons and azaleas thrive in this 0.4-hectare urban garden.
The site slopes down to a stream where primulas, hostas and other damp-loving plants
grow happily. Roses in beds and on archways make a striking contrast, as do the
rockeries. A number of the perennials and bulbs are grown for Shirley's enjoyment of
floral art. Ian has a comprehensive nursery stocked with dwarf rhododendrons — his
favourite.
Visits by appointment. Entry fee.

Maureen Ostler,
"Ostler's Gardens", Warwick Road, R.D.21, Stratford. **Tel:(06) 765 5611**
Ostler's Gardens cover a very large area and feature three equally big lakes. Rhododendrons and camellias are the predominant plantings and comprise a huge collection, a number of which are Ostler hybrids. Other trees include maples, magnolias, natives, cherry trees and conifers. Damp and shade plants grow around the water's edge. Fuchsias, lilies, begonias and waterlilies contribute to this all-year garden with a rural outlook and lovely vistas. Water birds can be seen on the lakes.
Open every weekend. Other times by appointment.

John and Elaine Nicholls,
"Woodhill" ("Chapman-Taylor Garden"),
Mountain Road, R.D.23, Stratford. **Tel:(06) 765 5497**
Probably best known as the Chapman-Taylor Garden, Woodhill comprises 0.8 hectares of English-styled woodland where many mature rhododendrons, azaleas, magnolias and camellias mixed with natives and deciduous trees, especially cherries and maples, grow in ideal conditions. Ferns and pongas have naturalised all over the garden, as have many spring bulbs and perennials. Herbs have their own dell. There are many precious plants in this old established garden.
The garden is open most days, but prior notice of visits, especially from groups, would be appreciated. Entry fee. Morning and afternoon teas available by prior arrangement. Toilets available. Accommodation for 8 people.

Mr and Mrs G. Marshall,
Stanley Road, R.D.24, Stratford. **Tel:(06) 762 8775**
Set on a level plateau, this large tranquil garden is surrounded by native bush, which attracts many birds. Selections of deciduous trees have been planted round the house in combination with conifers and natives. An assortment of herbaceous plants and bulbs flower well into summer. Brickwork edges many of the perennial beds and some cleverly placed local stones look like sculptures.
Visits by appointment. There is an art studio where visitors can purchase work by Mr and Mrs Marshall.

Gwyn Masters,
"Aramaunga", 669 Beaconsfield Road,
R.D.24, Stratford. **Tel:(06) 765 7604**
Aramaunga is a large woodland garden with many different areas and corners, linked by lawns and easily negotiated paths. Rhododendrons, azalea mollis, magnolias and maples predominate. A number of rock gardens overlook a lake which is fed by a stream with a bridge. Gwyn has a lovely collection of wisterias, some of which she has cleverly pruned into weeping forms; others climb trees along with clematis. Japanese lanterns and pieces of pottery nestled throughout the garden add interest, and the landscaping is a delight.
Visits by appointment. Please telephone early morning or evening. Entry fee.

Neville and Ruth Cleland,
Gordon Road, R.D.22, Stratford. **Tel:(06) 762 2720**
The Clelands started off growing only rhododendrons in their large garden but soon added other trees and shrubs, mainly camellias, magnolias, azaleas, natives, conifers

and ericas, along with many deciduous trees. There is also a collection of peonies. Ponds lined with bog plants create interest. There are many paths and interesting walks.
Visits by appointment. Visitors are welcome to bring lunch. Hot water available. Toilet available.

Jim and Molly Hopkirk,
"Maranui", R.D.22, Makahu, Stratford.   **Tel:(06) 762 3807**
Maranui consists of several hectares of woodland garden, some of it planted around 65 years ago. The new plantings are quite extensive, with many rhododendrons, azaleas, camellias, conifers, deciduous trees and natives. A delightful waterfall flows into a stream which runs through the garden, its banks lined with bog plants. This garden is also a haven for birds.
Open from dawn until dusk during October and November. At other times, visits by appointment. Visitors are welcome to bring lunch. Hot water can be supplied. Morning and afternoon teas can also be provided by prior arrangement. Toilet .

J. and R. Barrett,
"Tututawa", R.D.22, Stratford.   **Tel:(06) 762 7864**
A stream flows through these meandering, multi-level gardens of 2.4 hectares. Some areas are in woodland style, others contain water and bog gardens. Many cherry trees, maples, dogwoods and magnolias make a brilliant showing in springtime, to say nothing of the hundreds of rhododendrons. Many of these trees and shrubs have been grown from cuttings by the owners. The house is surrounded by a large herbaceous garden which is full of colour until the end of summer.
Garden open to the public in October and November. At other times by prior arrangement. Telephone evenings or early mornings please. Entry fee $5. Toilet.

Eva and Ray Frank,
"Klien Vale", R.D.22, Stratford.   **Tel:(06) 762 7833**
In this small garden one side has been terraced to eliminate the sudden drop. Eva is fond of camellias and she has quite a collection, as well as rhododendrons and roses. Bulbs have naturalised everywhere. Fuchsias are housed in a shelterhouse. The best time for viewing is mid August to February.
Visits by appointment.

Albert Marchant,
Cardiff Road, R.D.21, Stratford.
Postal address: 5 Climie Road, R.D.21, Stratford   **Tel:(06) 765 5409**
This steep hillside garden was terraced a number of years ago and fully planted with rhododendrons. Some of these are rare and special and were cultivated by the early rhododendron authority, Mr H. J. Marchant. Conifers are also planted throughout, especially a selection of redwoods.
Visits by appointment.

Maurie and Erica Jago,
"Merleswood", 7 Beaconsfield Road, Stratford.   **Tel:(06) 765 6484**
A large number of tall deciduous trees frame this country garden, including a specimen 70-year-old spreading elm which dominates one of the lawn areas. All of the

garden is easy walking and has views towards Mount Taranaki. A woodland is underplanted in a host of leafy plantings giving a cool feeling, while beds feature many perennials and roses, a favourite being the *rugosa* species because of their interesting hips. Logs and stumps have been used to edge paths and gardens. Erica has a collection of wisterias; these climb over pergolas, along a veranda and appear throughout the garden pruned as standards, while a hedge of Mexican orange blossom lines a fence beneath a row of *Prunus* 'Awanui'. Rhododendrons, maples, camellias and conifers also feature. The driveway is through a tunnel of trees of mixed planting and entry to the garden in early spring is greeted by a blanket of daffodils.
  Entry fee. Visits by appointment. Toilet. Picnics welcome.

John and Myra Bayly,
"Tranquility Garden", 12 Ahuroa Road
(Factory Number 757), 22 R.D., Stratford.   Tel:(06) 762 2833
Myra has developed her country garden in a 3-tier effect; tall trees create a woodland area, there are also small trees and shrubs, and low-growing plants act as ground covers. Plantings include natives, rhododendrons, azaleas, camellias, deciduous trees and lots of conifers (one of the favourites). Beds include many varieties of iris, lilies and mixed perennials. Climbers also feature. Easy walking paths and curving lawns join the different levels. Lots of seats are situated so that the visitor can enjoy the tranquillity or the lovely vistas. A small pond edged with damp foliage plants has a hump bridge over the middle.
  Picnics welcome. Toilet. Visits by appointment.

Jill Kuriger,
Waingongoro, R.D.21, Stratford.   Tel:(06) 765 5165
Rock plants and alpines, camellias, azaleas and rhododendrons grow at the Kuriger garden, along with deciduous trees. Underplantings of bulbs and perennials, bog plants, peonies and ferns flourish. Keen gardeners have planted so much there is no room for lawns and they have now got a 'starting house' filled with many pots of seeds and cuttings. Visitors will find something colourful here all year round.
  Visits by appointment.

R. and M. Dudli,
"Swiss Garten", Eltham Road, R.D.29, Kaponga.   Tel:(06) 274 5624
The delightful Swiss Garten has been developed from a steep swampy gully. It is now terraced, tracked, stepped and planted out in trees and shrubs. A summer garden with the emphasis on begonias, which always make a colourful display.
  Visits by appointment. Entry fee. Open to the public weekends only, from 1 January to the end of May. Other times by arrangement only.

Elaine and George Brewer,
"Craemona", 85 Ihaia Road, Opunake.   Tel:(06) 761 8498
Craemona is an old-fashioned garden with some big camellias and two protected trees, one a huge kowhai and the other a rata. There are bulbs everywhere during spring and the sunken fernery is quite unusual. The big attraction in Elaine's garden is the begonias; she has over 260 plants, a colourful sight from December through to March.
  Visits by appointment.

Hollard Gardens, Upper Manaia Road, Kaponga.
The Hollard Gardens, originally created by Mr and Mrs Bernard Hollard, are now run by the Queen Elizabeth II National Trust. Time is needed to fully appreciate this property. There are so many aspects to it, including a terrific collection of rhododendrons, azaleas, camellias, rare plants and trees. Old sections of the garden contain native woodland areas and newly planted sections have wide grass paths and curving borders. A swamp and bog garden is full of primulas, and wetland plants, trimmed azaleas and hedges, bulbs and perennials. Most of the trees and shrubs are named, which always adds interest, not only for the tourist but also for the gardener and horticulturist. The garden dates back to 1927, so there are some fine specimens to be seen.
Open every day except Christmas Day. Entry fee. For further information contact the curator, Mr Greg Rine, (06) 764 6544 or after hours 764 6616.

Beryl and Charlie Washer,
Marumarunui, R.D.31, Opunake.   **Tel:(06) 763 8700**
This very large and inviting garden has a stand of native bush with walks through it bordering one side. There is a magnificent copper beech tree in the centre of a large lawn and rhododendrons, camellias and azaleas surround the area. There are also lots of bulbs and perennials everywhere. The vistas at different corners of the garden are superb.
Groups of interested persons welcome by arrangement.

Tui and Kathryn Young,
"Pukekohatu", Waiteika Rd,
R.D.32, Opunake.   **Tel: (06) 761 7276**
"Pukekohatu" means stony hills, very appropriate for this part of the country and it is special to the Youngs as it is family tribal land. Features include a stairway leading to a gazebo smothered with clematis and surrounded with a variety of trees and shrubs, a pergola and fence made from macrocapa limbs which has pointers to an Agonis tree with perennials at one end, and a cherry "Hill" tree with miniature roses at the other. A childrens playground and garden with Sesame Street characters painted on fences, a sundial and bird bath surrounded with lavenders, and a three tier fountain with a buxus hedging, are also other interesting areas. Many native trees and shrubs are included in the plantings of this coastal garden.
Open to public 20–21 January 10.00 a.m. – 5.00 p.m. or by appointment at other times. Entry fee $3.

Ian and Judith Armstrong,
Eltham Road, Opunake.   **Tel:(06) 761 8052**
Strong sea winds are the deciding factor for planting in this large country garden, which presents a challenge tor the Armstrongs. Gently sloping lawns are edged with some mature trees and flower beds have mixed plantings.
Visits by appointment. Picnics in garden welcome. Toilet.

Ina Pickering,
54 Fox Street, Opunake.   **Tel:(06) 761 8850**
Salt-laden winds determine the choice of plant in this small urban seaside garden. Intensively planted with a mixture of trees, small shrubs and perennials, shadehouses add contrast with tender plants, particularly fuchsias, of which Ina is fond.
Visits by appointment.

Jim and Jeneane Feaver,
Opua Road, Opunake.   **Tel:(06) 761 8734**
Local stone has been used in a number of rock gardens here, where strong winds are a constant threat to this coastal country garden. Plantings behind a shelter of tall pohutukawa trees are of mixed rhododendrons, camellias, conifers, blossom trees, azaleas and roses, in beds and on a pergola. A sunken lawn area in one corner adds interest to the flat easy-walking paths and lawns.
Visits by appointment.

Andrew and Sharon Gooch,
Main South Road,
Rahotu, Opunake.   **Tel:(06) 763 8330**
Predominately a tree and shrub garden, this garden is very colourful in spring and has lovely autumn leaf colour. There are blossom trees, rhododendrons and camellias, many of which circle the whole section, and a special rare golden pine dominates one corner.
Visits by appointment.

John and Phyllis Malcolm,
18 Tempsky Road, Okaiawa.   **Tel:(06) 272 6663**
Phyllis describes her garden, built on a sloping area overlooking a large lake, as one which has 'just grown'. She is a floral artist who also 'dabbles in dried flowers', and so she usually plants with these interests in mind. Many larger trees and shrubs complement her garden scene, which has as a focal point a long bridge crossing the lake.
Visits by appointment.

Mr and Mrs A. P. Gamlin and Mrs V. Joyce,
"Camellia Glen", Lower Glen Road,
R. D.28, Manaia.   **Tel: home (06) 274 8748; nursery 274 8372**
A large collection of camellias are dotted over a wide area in this combined garden and nursery. The best time for visiting is between May and mid October, with the peak of the flowering season at the beginning of August.
The nursery is open from Easter to Labour Weekend, 7 days a week, 9.30 a.m. to 4.30 p.m. For large groups, prior notice would be appreciated. Visitors are welcome to bring lunch. Toilets available.

Carol and John Lynskey,
"The Lynskeys",
Oeo Rd, R.D.28, Manaia.   **Tel: (06) 274 8700**
Surrounded by flat farmland this ¾-acre garden has been growing since the mid 1980s. Over this time various rooms have developed with plantings of trees, shrubs, roses and lots of garden goodies that mainly take care of themselves. Best time is spring — October to December — when early bulbs appear. Autumn deciduous tree colour is good from May to August.
Visits by appointment around these times. Picnics welcome. Hot water and toilet available.

H. N. and S. Mills,
63 Ngatai Street, Manaia.   Tel:(06) 274 8380

An interesting, colourful town section closely planted with beds of roses, rhododendrons, camellias, bulbs and perennials. Pots of succulents thrive in sunny corners and
an effectively planted bank and orchids in a shelterhouse, together with many fuchsias, complete the garden.

Visits by appointment.

Jenny and Guy Oakley,
Lower Normanby Road, Manaia.   Tel:(06) 274 8060

Although buffered by coastal winds, Jenny has managed to grow a wide selection of
cottage plants in this large country garden designed around family living. Constructions of brick and timber work support raised beds of flowers and herbs, and form
steps and archways creating an overall delightful picture. Different levels also add
interest.

Visits by appointment.

Arna Malone and James Malone,
"Blue Bonnet Cottage", 34 Hunter Street, Normanby.   Tel: (06) 272 8240

Arna and her son James have developed their 1-acre garden on a level site at the edge
of the village of Normanby. Surrounded on all sides by tall hedges and trees, the beds
are planted in a comprehensive collection of colourful perennials, herbs and small
shrubs. Grass paths and lawns make for easy viewing while a small pond and many
individual pottery pieces by local potter Marilyn Dreaver feature. A nursery of display
beds set in gravel paths contain plants seen in the garden.

Toilet. Open 7 days a week, 10.a .m. to 6 p.m.

Marion and John Murphy,
"Riverlea", Wirihana Road, Hawera.   Tel:(06) 278 7864

Garden design is important in this large country garden. Gently sloping lawns
are edged by curving raised flower beds. Roses, both modern and heritage
varieties, are in beds, over archways and on pergolas, blending with many
perennials in colour combinations. Marion also has a collection of lavenders
and herbs. Surrounding the whole section is a mixture of natives, camellias,
rhododendrons, azaleas, deciduous trees and cherry trees. A considerable
amount of brickwork adds character in this all-year, colourful and tranquil
garden.

*Open October to April. Visits by appointment. Entry fee $2. Five minutes from SH
45 and SH 3.*

Mr and Mrs R. A. Corrigan,
"Parkhill", P.O. Box 448, Hawera.   Tel:(06) 278 4223

Parkhill is a large garden which obtains its woodland atmosphere from its many well
established trees underplanted with azaleas, camellias, rhododendrons, bulbs and perennials. A bush walk on an easy track is interesting. A large lawn gives a feeling of
space, and beds of roses add colour and fragrance.

Visits by appointment.

Roma and Leo Park,
"Kauris", 32 Douglas Street, Hawera.   **Tel:(06) 278 5437**
An attractive and colourful road-front garden frames this level urban section. Groups
of conifers, succulents and lantanas in a raised area shield the lawns from the street.
One lawn area has a raised section, with a sunken corner for interest. Brick and broken concrete has been used for raised flower beds, a courtyard and a moongate. A
collection of pelargoniums is colourful and as the name suggests, a few mighty kauri
dominate this garden.
Visits by appointment. Donations to the SPCA.

Ron and Jacklyn Edgcombe,
"Ti-Maru", 41 Cameron Street, Hawera.   **Tel:(06) 278 6360**
Large trees surround two sides of this 100-year-old home, with one side having a cool
walkway winding through it. Large local rocks have been used for raised flower and
shrub beds. The expansive lawns are on two levels and an attractive brick herbery is
interesting.
Visits by appointment.

Jene and Charles Holloway,
5 Gladstone Street, Hawera.   **Tel:(06) 278 4265**
Small level urban section with camellias and modern roses. A cool corner with mixed
plantings of trees and shrubs.
Visits by appointment.

King Edward Park,
Hawera.
This spacious area, almost in the centre of town, is surrounded by big trees and attractive garden beds. During spring, the rhododendrons, camellias and roses form a colourful display. The rose beds are set out in a formal pattern surrounded by a low
hedge; other roses climb over a long pergola. There is a Chinese Garden in the design
of the Willow Pattern; a very tranquil place to linger. Annual and bulb beds, also
surrounded by low hedges, are set out in a formal pattern. These are a blaze of colour
throughout spring and summer. At one end of the garden is a children's playground.
Open daily.

Mr and Mrs L. V. Walker,
304 High Street, Hawera.   **Tel:(06) 278 6237**
Large cherry trees make a great spring showing on this 0.8-hectare town site. There
are about 150 roses and approximately 60 camellias. Large beds of annuals are set out
in expansive lawns. A mixture of other trees and shrubs surround the garden.
Visits by appointment.

Mrs G. Jones,
"Hurleyville", R.D.2, Patea.   **Tel:(06) 273 4269**
A wide rural view adds charm to this large garden. Conifers, camellias, rhododendrons, magnolias and rose beds, together with perennials and annuals, ensure something is in flower all the time, but Hurleyville is especially fine during spring and
summer.
Visits by appointment.

Rudi Milesi,
"Chriesi Wald", 7 Hadfield Street, Patea.   **Tel:(06) 273 8171**
The name in Swiss means 'cherrywood', and on this small town site there are no less than 30 cherry trees, as well as 50 camellias. An intensively planted garden which has colour all year, Chriesi Wald is landscaped in small sections divided by arches, small walls and doors.
Visits by appointment.

Jeanette and Laurie Gibbs,
170 Egmont Street, Patea.   **Tel:(06) 273 8674**
There are three large Norfolk pines and an equally large pohutakawa tree in this big, mixed-level, urban garden. Other trees include natives, conifers, eucalyptus trees, rhododendrons and camellias, and small trees and shrubs are underplanted and edged with cottage plants. A courtyard has a blue and white theme in raised flower beds while other raised beds use local shell/rock for an interesting effect. Steps and grass walkways connect expansive lawns. Pottery pieces and driftwood to be seen in many corners.
Visits by appointment.

Wanganui/Taihape

"Westerly Walks"

The following 4 gardens form a group called "Westerly Walks". Morning, after-noon teas and lunches by arrangement. Entry fee to each garden. Accommodation can be arranged.

Donald and Jocelyn Walkinton,
"Puketiro", R.D.2, Waverley.   **Tel:(06) 346 5374**
Created on a sloping site with a spacious lawn, this is a new garden facing north, in harmony with the rural view. There is a large collection of camellias, also blossom trees, rhododendrons and proteas underplanted with perennials and bulbs.
Visits by appointment.

Norman and Marsaile Walkinton,
"Belmont", R.D.2, Waverley.   **Tel:(06) 346 5114**
To appreciate its long, very colourful and interestingly planted driveway, visitors should walk to this garden, which surrounds an historic 112-year-old house. The many trees, old and new, are underplanted with perennials, bulbs and ground covers. One sum-mertime feature is a long white rose bed. A collection of native trees and shrubs creates a woodland feeling and the lawns are extensive.
Visits by appointment.

Jill and Gerald Hare,
"Te Rama", Nukumaru, R.D.17, Waitotora.   **Tel: (06) 342 3837**
Rustic seats throughout this large country garden are situated so visitors can enjoy the long pleasant vistas at every corner. Railway sleepers and split posts are used exten-sively for banks and step constructions. The flower beds have a wide range of plants mixed with trees and shrubs. A rhododendron dell at the end of the section has a

white theme and tall mamanga tree ferns along a bank are contrasting features. Roses grow on archways and along fence lines. The garden has been designed with the activities of a young family in mind.
Visits by appointment.

Ross and Joan Richardson,
"Wereroa", P.O. Box 17, Waitotara.   **Tel:(06) 346 5026**
This spacious, rustic garden, with big lawns and beds of perennials and roses, is still being expanded. A steep bank has been intensively planted with species our native birds appreciate. At the bottom is a natural stream with a bridge crossing to an area of large tree ferns and fast growing native trees and shrubs. There are wide grass paths and steps all through this area. This garden needs time to explore.
Visits by appointment.

Heather and John Dickie,
"Hayes", Karahaki Road, Waverley.   **Tel:(06) 346 5080**
A well-grown collection of native trees with other deciduous and blossom trees surround this large country garden with its split-level expansive lawns. Many grouped rhododendrons grow in a woodland dell and others throughout the garden blend with camellias and azalea mollis. These bring springtime colour, along with thousands of daffodils. Roses, a lavender hedge and a catmint hedge add contrast. Autumn brings beautiful colour with the many cherry trees.
Visits by appointment.

Mary-Ann and Roger Dickie,
"Awatea", Main North Road, Waverley.   **Tel:(06) 346 5329**
Designed for family living, the garden at Awatea has many facets. In one corner a woodland area has been created, with a collection of rhododendrons and camellias. Mary-Ann is fond of cottage plants and grows everlasting flowers and ornamental corn, etc. Old-fashioned roses are another favourite, and the garden is generally developing on old-world lines.
Visits by appointment.

Sue and Richard White,
"Rosemount", Waverley Beach Road, Waverley.   **Tel:(06) 346 5010**
The swift flowing Wairoa Stream passes through this large, wandering coastal country garden. Gently sloping expansive lawns fall towards the stream that is edged on the house side by a large garden mass planted in perennials, mainly in blue, yellow and white. On the other side it is fully planted in camellias, mixed with a variety of perennials and small shrubs. Elsewhere, flower gardens have mixed plantings, there being a big collection of Michaelmas daisies. Conifers give shelter, contrast and year-round colour. Blossom trees in outside paddocks give an extended feeling. This garden was originally planted by Diana Jackson.
Visits by appointment.

Harold and Jocelyn Symes, "Haurere", R.D.2, Waverley. Tel:(06) 346 5154
Facing north on a slope with lovely views, this garden grows rhododendrons, camellias, blossom trees, roses and perennials. Jocelyn plants annuals for summer showing. Best time for viewing is from the beginning of October until the end of February.
Visits by appointment.

Barry Pearce,
"Ashley Park", SH3, Waitotora.   **Tel:(06) 346 5917**
Ashley Park has a large lake with a walkway around it surrounded by mixed plantings of trees, shrubs and ground covers. Spring is colourful with camellias, cherry trees, rhododendrons and many more flowers, while autumn is full of leaf colour. There are still areas in development and many varieties of birds in cages can be seen.
Picnic area with table and chairs. Accommodation and camping facilities available. Antique shop with light lunches and Devonshire teas.

Rob and Juliette Handley,
Rangiatau West Road, Maxwell, R.D. Waitotara.   **Tel:(06) 342 3844**
Native pigeons enjoy the masses of berries produced by holly trees lining the driveway to this large, split-level country garden. Mature trees, including very large rhododendrons, shelter one side of the section. Thyme steps, cottage plants, climbers and a collection of old-fashioned roses feature. Juliette has a garden of plants especially for picking and cuttings for new plants. In the surrounding paddocks, Rob has planted a wide range of trees, as well as a field of walnuts for commercial use. There is also a symmetrical European styled gravel courtyard with a formal Lutons pond and three other ponds dropping into each other.
Visits by appointment during weekends only.

Iain Elliot,
"Punga Park", R.D.4, Wanganui.   **Tel:(06) 342 9860**
This sloping site of approximately 0.6 hectares with a woodland garden has numerous mature native trees sheltering a large collection of rhododendrons, azaleas, camellias and many shade-loving perennials. Other new areas have walkways through them, and here again rhododendrons, camellias and blossom trees feature. Splendid views.
Visits by appointment.

John and Rosemary Deroles,
Tuamata, R.D.1, Wanganui.   **Tel:(06) 342 1892**
Rosemary's garden is colourful and most of her plantings are chosen for their picking value. Bulbs, perennials, ground covers and flowers, all suitable for drying, are some of the treasures to be found. Camellias and roses occur frequently throughout the garden, which offers a spectacular view towards the sea.
Visits by appointment.

Bushy Park, Bushy Park Conservation Trust,
Rangitatau East Road, Kai-iwi.   **Tel:(06) 342 9879**
Postal address: Bushy Park Lodge, Kai-iwi R.D.8, Wanganui.
Surrounding the lodge, this park-like garden of 10.5 hectares is a mixture of exotic
and native trees, and a haven for a great variety of native birds. Large lawns on
different levels blend into the bush, and there are walking tracks throughout. An
arboretum is planted with native trees and shrubs not common to this area. To add
interest and colour, there are perennial and bulb beds and a few exotic shrubs. Behind
the lodge is 98 hectares of bush with native trees identified and a huge Northern rata.
The lodge and grounds are open from 10 a.m. to 5 p.m. daily. Entry fee. Toilet
available. The historic homestead has accommodation for 16 people in 6 rooms and
community cooking facilities. For further information write to the postal address
above, or telephone.

Mrs Vonnie Cave,
Seafield, R.D.4, Wanganui.   **Tel:(06) 345 8326**
Camellias figure prominently in this coastal garden and some of them are rather special. Beds of perennials, annuals, herbaceous plants, cacti and a large collection of
succulents make this a colourful and diverse garden. Several shade houses are home
to cyclamens, begonias and other rare and tender plants. Time is needed to see it all.
Visits by appointment. Entry fee.

Virginia Lake Reserve,
Great North Road, Wanganui.
An area at the top of Street John's Hill, owned and administered by the Wanganui City
Council, this reserve has a large natural lake surrounded by established trees, shrubs
and bog plants. There are easy-walking tracks which provide many good views and
lots of shady picnic spots. Camellias grouped together make a handsome spring showing
and rhododendrons also flourish here. Beds of bulbs, perennials and many annuals
enhance the summer display, along with the waterlilies on the lake. The Winter Garden conservatory is home to many tender plants, including cyclamen, orchids and
numerous ferns. It is open Monday to Saturday, from 10 a.m. to 4 p.m., and on
Sundays from 10 a.m. to 5 p.m. Around the lawn areas a number of bronze statues are
to be found. An aviary, constructed to an unusual design, is another feature popular
with children. Alongside this is a natural amphitheatre where concerts are held.
Accessible daily. Toilets available.

Bason Botanical Reserve,
Rapanui Road, Wanganui.
This 25.6 hectares of parkland is free for all to enjoy. Most of it can be driven around.
The terrain is varied, with gullies and lakes. The plantings are also varied, including
natives, palms and exotic trees. An unusual and interesting display house, made of
brick and glass, is home to tender plants. This is open weekdays from 10 a.m. to 4
p.m., and at weekends and public holidays from 2 p.m. to 4 p.m. There is a developing
native aboretum, a fern gully with a walk through it, and many other additions. The
homestead is set in a sheltered cottage garden with camellias and old-world plants.
There are collections of the protea family, rhododendrons, camellias, azaleas, maples,
magnolias, viburnums and conifers. This developing park is supported by Friends of
Bason Society, Wanganui, and administered by the Wanganui City Council.
Accessible at all times. Toilets available.

Joan Morrell,
82 Parsons Street, Springvale, Wanganui.　　　　　　**Tel:(06) 345 0746**
Birds enjoy this peaceful woodland city garden. Small ponds full of fish are edged with damp-loving plants. Seats are scattered throughout the garden inviting visitors to sit and enjoy the tranquillity. Joan is probably New Zealand's best known bronze sculptress and has a studio in the garden, available to view by arrangement.
　　Visits by appointment. Entry fee for studio. Picnic lunch in garden welcome.

Brian and Louise Herlihy,
"Almondale", 110 Riverbank Road, Wanganui.　　　　　**Tel:(06) 343 6044**
Almondale is a large level country garden on the edge of the city. The original design is an early Buxton creation and has had a series of additions. A circle of large shelter trees has resulted in a woodland garden and many camellias, rhododendrons, azaleas and cherry trees give dappled light to hostas and a variety of foliage plants. An enclosed formally laid out rose garden is planted in old-fashioned roses and ramblers. Many perennials and annuals self-seed all over the garden. An orchard provides a big selection of fruit and lots of native birds frequent the garden. As a floral artist, being able to pick flowers and foliage all year is important to Louise.
　　Visits by appointment mid October to mid December. Teas and light lunches available by arrangement. Toilet.

Margaret and Maurice O'Connell,
54 Eastown Road, Wanganui.　　　　　　　　　**Tel:(06) 343 6295**
It is hard to imagine that you are in the centre of a city in this very large garden surrounded by mature trees, both native and exotic. There are extensive lawns, beds of perennials, roses and foliage plants, cool woodland and enclosed intimate areas. A paved semicircular courtyard edged with old-fashioned roses is designed for outdoor living. The fruit orchard also adds to the features and a new bog section is under construction. Autumn brings brilliant colour with so many big deciduous trees. Seats for resting are everywhere.
　　Visits by appointment all year. Picnics welcome. Hot water available. Toilet.

"Wanganui River Gardens"

The following three gardens can be visited in a day trip from the Paddle Wheeler Otunui on the Wanganui River in association with Holly Lodge. Wine tasting and refreshments also available. For enquiries and bookings telephone (06) 343 9344.

Russell and Janice Gaisford,
"Wairere", Papaiti Road, Wanganui.　　　　　　　**Tel:(06) 342 5823**
This large country garden has tall trees protecting a considerable collection of camellias, magnolias and beds of perennials and roses. A sunken courtyard designed for family living has white roses for interest and a small pond as a central focal point in a large sweeping lawn. Fantail pigeons and doves share the garden with native birds. A picking garden for dried flower outlets and fresh flowers is an attractive addition. Gherkins are grown and are available for purchase fresh from January to March or bottled all year. A haha along one side of the garden gives an uninterrupted view of the countryside. Janice has a shop stocked with bunches, baskets and bouquets of her dried

flowers. A deep gully on one side is being developed as a bog area along a waterway.
Open weekends or by appointment. Particularly pretty during the orchid and
camellia season.

Colin and Kath Campbell,
"Te Korito", Papaiti Road, Wanganui.   **Tel:(06) 342 5814**
This garden, designed on top of a rise, enjoys a fine view down the Wanganui River.
The driveway is through huge chestnut trees underplanted with masses of bluebells,
and they also shelter many camellias, rhododendrons, cherry trees and native trees.
One side has a stand of native trees with a path through and beds of perennials, roses,
bulbs and ground covers occur throughout the garden forming rooms. Native birds are
plentiful all year. Easy walking. Best time winter and spring.
Visits by appointment. Picnics welcome. Hot water available. Toilet. Colin has a
tree nursery stocked with varieties suitable for farm plantings.

Jenny and Charles Jackson,
"Ohorere", Papaiti Road, Wanganui.   **Tel:(06) 342 5848**
Delightful views of the Wanganui River from the house and a low level lawn are some
of the features in this large country riverside garden. An enormous liliodendron at the
entrance shelters a host of camellias, rhododendrons and azaleas elsewhere beds of
old-fashioned roses, modern roses and perennials flourish. A natural gully with two
springs forming ponds and a waterway beneath a stand of native trees, is a cool and
tranquil area, easy-walking paths wind throughout. Many dahlias and cannas add to
the summer colour.
Visits by appointment. Picnics welcome. Perennials and produce for sale. Devon-
shire teas if required

Margaret and Murray Carey,
75a Virginia Road, Wanganui.   **Tel:(06) 345 5086**
As a landscape designer, form and flow is important to Margaret. Designed around
family living, this interesting garden on the edge of the city has a very strong influence
of native plants. The large canopy trees, small grasses, flaxes, ground covers and
climbers blend happily together with collections of perennials, roses and exotic trees.
Winding paths thread through thickets and there is plenty of bird life.
Visits by appointment all year.

Peter and Dinny Brosnahan,
"Birch Lea", Station Road, Westmere, Wanganui.   **Tel:(06) 345 8068**
This large level country garden has a cool woodland area for its driveway that extends
into the garden itself. Many large trees, including a 90-year-old pohutakawa and a
kauri tree, shelter collections of rhododendrons, camellias and azaleas. Clipped box
hedges, beds of roses and perennials, and rustic fences of old posts and battens create
intimate areas. And a sunken lawn in one corner, archways and a small pond are just
some of the attractive features. Autumn produces lovely colours. Dinny has designed
the garden from the windows of the house so as to have a pleasing picture from within.
Visits from appointment.

Kevin and Sheryl Gedye,
"Wairimu", 1671 Blueskin Road, R.D. 1, Wanganui.   **Tel:(06) 345 0814**
Wairimu is a 2-tier garden consisting of a large, level upper area and a deep terraced gully joined by a native walkway. The upper level features a rose arbor, circular garden, cottage garden beds, archways and a semi-formal modern rose garden. The gully features edgings of local shell rock and sleepers with plantings of natives, colourful clumps of perennials and damp-loving plants, along with shady foliage species, around several large ponds fed by a natural spring. Tall tree ferns tower overhead and shelter the area, which has helped to create a micro-climate. Many rhododendrons and conifers.

Open every day, October to end of Easter, at other times by appointment only. Ample seating for picnics and coach turning. Toilet. Plants for sale. Teas by arrangement.

Miles and Jocelyn Bockett,
24 Taranaki Street, Wanganui.   **Tel:(06) 345 3247**
A hillside, terraced, city garden with winding paths threading through the mass-planted beds sheltered beneath many silver birch trees. Lots of old roses, herbs, perennials, bulbs and ground covers feature. At the lower level, the tall trees of various species create a woodland garden where the bog areas are planted in leafy plantings. There are also fruit trees. A wild garden and a swamp area are under construction. In the front of the section is a bricked courtyard circled by roses and perennials and self-seeding annuals. Daffodils are to the fore in early spring.

Plants for sale. Teas by arrangement. Visits by appointment. Entry fee.

Clive and Nicki Higgie,
"Fernwood", 223 Denlari Road, Fordell, Wanganui.   **Tel:(06) 342 7857**
The theme and intention in this rather unusual large country garden is to develop a sub-tropical garden with a wide range of plant forms. Many different varieties of palms, bamboos, cycads, cacti and tree ferns are planted around the house, while others are in shelterhouses. Echiums, aloes, bromeliads, sedges, agaves and grasses blend with rare trees and shrubs, including native and exotic species. A large developing gully is planted with avenues of palms amongst trees and shrubs. Grass walkways wind throughout the whole area and a long hump bridge connects the two sides.

Visits by appointment.

Barry Nixon,
"Sedgebrook", 31 Sedgebrook Street, Wanganui.   **Tel:(06) 343 7394**
A wide variety of trees and shrubs is one of the interesting features in this woodland city garden with the Nixon Creek framing two sides. A flat lawn slopes down to a tranquil lawn edged with damp-loving plants. Underplanting of large trees includes a comprehensive collection of hostas, primulas, hellebores and ferns. Spring is colourful with camellias, magnolias, bulbs and blossom trees, while glorious autumn colour is produced from maples, persimmon, ornamental quince and blossom trees. A magnificent walnut tree in front of the house looks like a protective umbrella. At the entrance, Barry has built an unusual bamboo Japanese gateway and there are large paving slabs of local stone.

Visits by appointment. Barry's son Greg has a specialist perennial nursery in the garden. It is open weekends 9 a.m. to 5p.m.

Mr Allan James, R.D.5, Wanganui.   **Tel:(06) 342 5791**
On this level site the garden blends with a block of native bush in a deep gully along-side. The view looking down into the huge trees is most unusual. Birds enjoy the whole environment. In the garden, many rhododendrons, camellias, magnolias and conifers have bulbs, perennials and ground covers naturalising beneath their branches. *Visits by appointment.*

Mrs Joan Harris,
"Rosehills", R.D. Mangamahu.   **Tel:(06) 342 2841**
Essentially a tree and shrub garden, Rosehills, as the name implies, is filled with roses of the modern varieties. Complementing these are numerous weeping trees of many species, all grouped together to give a most dramatic effect. In addition to cherry, beech, silver birch, elm and mulberry trees, the garden contains many magnolias, conifers, camellias and rhododendrons. Best time for viewing is from the beginning of August through to March or April.
Visits by appointment. Entry fee. A nursery attached specialises in roses and weeping trees for purchase.

Sarah and John Vickers,
"Tutaenui", Woodleigh Farm, R.D.2, Marton.   **Tel:(06) 327 7280**
This spacious garden is designed for family living. There is a large collection of irises and roses, modern and old-fashioned, also camellias, rhododendrons and a selection of the protea family. Many perennials and bulbs flourish on these acres. There is a woodland garden, a wonderful iris walk, and in a developing area a small pond is the focal point. Best time for viewing this garden is from the end of October until the end of November.
Open from October to December daily; other times by appointment. Entry fee. Morning and afternoon teas can be provided by prior arrangement only. John will arrange visits to historic homesteads in the area.

Robert and Jan Young,
"Craig Lea", Griffin Rd,
R.D.2, Marton.   **Tel: (06) 327 6405**
A camellia and azalea lined drive welcomes you to this established garden. Standing sentinel over the surrounding native bush is a majestic rimu tree. This bush creates a backdrop for rhododendrons, a wide range of trees, shrubs, hostas and specialist perennials giving colour and texture in every season, and providing a haven for native birds. A collection of Chinese *Camellia reticulata* is a feature of Craig Lea in late winter and early spring.
Visits by appointment. Entry fee.

The Marshall Family,
"The Ridges", State Highway 1,
R.D.1, Marton.   **Tel:(06) 327 8484/Fax:(06) 327 8279**
This garden is a delight to wander through. The driveway is planted in rhododendrons and camellias, underplanted with many bulbs and perennials, making a pretty and colourful entry. Elsewhere there are rhododendrons, camellias, azaleas, blossom trees and specimen trees, evergreen and deciduous. Many hundreds of special bulbs planted

The Ridges

GARDEN & NURSERY

Specialising in unusual perennials and bulbs, and old favourites.

10 kilometres north of Marton on S.H.1.

in groups create mass displays. Perennials are everywhere, and a feature is a formal sunken garden. From the large lawn there is a wide rural view. It takes time to see this garden. A nursery has a large variety of interesting plants and garden ornaments for sale (a mail-order catalogue is available).

Open every day, 10 a.m. to 4.30 p.m., 20 September to 30 November and 20 March to 30 April. Closed for Easter. Groups at other times by appointment. Entry fee, but children free. Toilet available. Morning, afternoon teas and lunches are available for groups by prior arrangement (minimum 10 people).

Steuart and Linda Welch,
"Cannock Wood Nursery", Warrens Road, Marton.   Tel:(06) 327 6507

Unusual and rare trees, shrubs and perennials are in the nursery and growing in the private country garden of the Welchs'. A pond and damp area is under development where relevant plants will be seen. A fine collection of hollies is a speciality.

Open every Sunday, although a phone call would be appreciated.

Joe and Ali Fullerton-Smith,
"Linkwood", Galpin Road, Marton.   Tel:(06) 327 6523

Family living and pets were considered during the development of this large, contoured country garden. A stand of native bush nearby provides a lovely backdrop and brings a wealth of native birds to the garden. Extensive lawns are edged with flower beds and a mixture of trees, shrubs and roses.

Visits by appointment. Picnic lunches welcome. Toilet.

Judy and Bob Christie,
"Mungoven", 20 Tutaenui Road, Marton.   **Tel:(06) 327 8343**
Group plantings, local rocks, huge boulders and unusually shaped clipped hedges are just a few delightful features to be seen in this well-planted, artistically landscaped country garden, at the end of a long avenue of trees. A tremendous collection of conifers, ground covers, rhododendrons, camellias, azaleas, ericas and native trees blend in different areas, such as a bog garden, woodland garden, pond garden, shrubbery and a shelterhouse. Paths connect sections throughout. Spring brings bulbs and blossoms, there are roses and annuals for summer, and autumn has a delightful mixture of leaf colour. An all-year garden with lots to see.
Visits by appointment. Entry fee.

Margaret and Jaff Frederick,
"Springfield", Union line, Marton.   **Tel:(06) 327 7561**
Twin ponds at the bottom of a gully have been skillfully edged with zigzagging paths and mass planted in a mixture of trees, shrubs, perennials, bulbs and ground covers. Rustic archways, fences and pergolas support climbers and roses. Around the house, on a higher level, expansive lawns are edged with flower beds and a large number of specimen trees. A disused swimming pool has been converted to a sunken courtyard featuring potted plants, seats and archways. This large all-year garden with lovely vistas and plenty of colour needs time to see. Wonderful rural outlook.
Visits by appointment. Entry fee.

Wendy and Alan Willis,
"Earlstoun", Greatford, SH1, Marton.   **Tel:(06) 327 8410**
A pan of water beneath the surface has meant that the flower beds had to be raised for drainage in this large, colourful and restful country garden surrounded by mature trees (which produce delightful autumn leaf colour). Curving flower beds have mixed plantings of smaller trees, shrubs and many perennials, bulbs and ground covers. A considerable amount of brickwork and the use of railway sleepers add contrast. Expansive lawns have group and specimen trees, while in the outer paddocks more trees have been planted to give depth. Lovely vistas everywhere.
Visits by appointment. Entry fee.

Jim and Diana Howard,
"Westoe Woodland Garden and Nursery",
R.D.1, Marton.   **Tel:(06) 327 6350**
A 'four-seasons' garden, Westoe is a large gracious country garden (situated 8 km north of Bulls on the Feilding Road) surrounding the historic Howard homestead (*c.* 1874). A collection of beautiful mature trees, native and exotic, combines with plantings of woodland perennials and bulbs. Birds abound everywhere in this tranquil setting and the garden can be enjoyed throughout the year. A nursery sells plants potted from many of the species found in the garden.
The garden is open every Tuesday to Saturday from 10 a.m. to 4 p.m. (other days by arrangement). Private tours available by prior arrangement. Entry fee. Picnickers welcome.

Madeline Smith,
"Taratanui", 31 Armagh Terrace, Marton.　　　**Tel:(06) 327 7106**
Entrance to this level, compactly planted, brick walled and paved urban garden with no room for lawn is through an interesting courtyard containing many potted plants, climbers and cool leafy trees and shrubs. Gardens are edged with bricks and stones, mass planted in a large collection of bush, climbing and miniature roses blending together with an equally large collection of perennials, herbs and ground covers. Surrounding the walls are rhododendrons, camellias, azaleas and deciduous trees. A small pond with a hump bridge, many well-placed seats to rest on and a picking garden feature, with flowers suitable for drying and with perfumes. Madeline has a fine selection of lavenders and scented geraniums.
Visits by appointment. Entry fee. Plants for sale.

Selwyn and Pat Lawrence,
No. 4 Rangatira Road, Hunterville.　　　**Tel:(06) 322 8214**
A small colourful urban garden with a wide range of plantings. Features include a woodland section, white garden, small pond set in a gravel garden mass planted with cottage plants, self-seeding annuals and roses. Closely planted, there is no room for lawn. A shadehouse shelters tender plants and seedlings, while a number of caged birds add interest and constant song. Many container plants add to this delightful easy-walking garden.
Open 1 October to 31 May, 7 days a week. Entry fee.

Judy and Gerry Scully,
"Raumai Grange Lavender Farm",
Parewanui Road, Bulls.　　　**Tel:(06) 322 0953/Mobile: 025 471959**
Around 6 acres of lavenders, including many varieties, are the feature here, alongside a large level country garden surrounding a house built in 1860. A solid grove of tall elm trees shelter one side of the section and beds of old-fashioned perennials set off sweeping lawns. A stable shop has a selection of gifts and Devonshire teas are served on rustic tables and long stools beneath the lavender-lined ceiling. Nursery stocked with lavenders and old-fashioned perennials.
Entry fee $4. Peak time mid December to mid January. Ample parking. Homestay. Picnics. Catering for functions. Bookings essential. 5 km from Bulls.

Christopher and Susanna Grace,
"Rathmoy", Rangitira Road,
Hunterville.　　　**Tel:(06) 322 8334/Fax: (06)322 8380**
Several large ponds are a focal point in this park-like, spacious country garden. Wide sweeping lawns have borders billowing with old roses, perennials, bulbs and masses of interesting trees. Rhododendrons, camellias and azaleas are to the fore in spring and autumn has a delightful range of leaf colour. There is a considerable amount of brickwork, including terraces, archways, bridges and walls forming small and intimate enclosed gardens. Unusual garden containers display a variety of plants. There are spectacular vistas in every corner. The vege garden blends into the overall design. A collection of animals including a donkey, kuni kuni pigs, black sheep and even a

llama live together, and bird song is constant — natives as well as fantail pigeons, numerous ducks and a white swan. This easy-walking garden takes time to view. *Open September to December, 10 a.m. to 5 p.m. Other times by appointment. Entry fee, children free. Luncheons and teas by arrangement. Large groups welcome, but please notify of visit. Situated on Rangitira Road off SH1 in the centre of Hunterville.*

Mrs June Rowe,
"Merchiston", R.D.1, Marton.   **Tel:(06) 322 8090**
To reach this garden you must travel a long wooded driveway through huge oaks, chestnuts and conifers, beneath which the ground has become naturalised with hellebores, bluebells, daffodils and ferns. The garden surrounds an historic house. The sweeping level lawns are accented by specimen trees, also groupings of camellias and rhododendrons. Adjoining the main garden is a natural woodland area with a large lake, where swans and ducks are resident. A long bridge and an old river canoe are features here. Many climbing vines twine round the blossom trees.

Groups only please, and by appointment, from the beginning of September until the end of March. Includes viewing of historic house. Bookings must be made well in advance. Entry fee goes to the Hunterville Street John Ambulance.

Liz and David Buchanan,
"Cairnmuir", SH2, Mangaweka.   **Tel:(06) 382 5878**
Masses of trees of many different species surround this large country garden developed on a hillside. A woodland area, damp bog garden filled with colour damp-loving plants, beds of modern roses, raised flower beds and a large pond area feature. Collections of clematis, with a number of other climbers such as roses, wisteria, vitus, lapageria and akebia quinata, are to be seen. An unusual courtyard is delightful and many delphiniums planted with 'Iceberg' roses make quite a showing in summer. Being able to pick flowers all year is of prime importance to Liz. Native birds abound and autumn here has glorious colour because of the variety of deciduous and blossom trees and the variety of conifers. Spring brings rhododendrons, camellias, azaleas and thousands of daffodils. An easy-walking all-year garden.

Open weekends from Labour Weekend to the end of April. Other times by appointment. Entry fee. Homestay for 4 people.

Kristin and Bunny Gorringe,
Kawhatau Valley Road, Mangaweka, Taihape.   **Tel:(06) 382 5721**
A large country garden that has a comprehensive collection of trees surrounding all sides, in the garden section and the adjoining paddocks. Extensive sweeping lawns on different levels have beds of mixed perennials, old roses, bulbs and ground covers. One side is woodland underplanted with lots of green leafy species. A huge walnut tree is a dominant feature, while an enclosed interestingly designed vege, herb and berry garden surrounded by fencing and clipped hedgings is quite different. Many tall rhododendrons and camellias start the spring flowering off and there is interest right through to the brilliant display of autumn tree colours. A number of natives helps the abundant bird population. Terrific views down to the Kawhatau valley and river, the steep gorge walls and beyond.

Visits by appointment. Entry fee.

Bessie and Ian Gordon,
"Ben Moi", R.D.4, Taihape.   Tel:(06) 388 1554
Ben Moi has been planted out following the natural contours of the site; from flat to
sloping, with a gully. Deciduous trees and conifers have created a woodland area
surrounding a large pond, which is home to swans, ducks and bog and water plants.
Elsewhere, rhododendrons camellias and blossom trees are all underplanted with per-
ennials and bulbs. This garden needs time to see it properly.
Visits by appointment.

Ron and Helen Gordon,
"Rongoiti Gardens", R.D.1,Taihape.   Tel:(06) 388 7866
This is a large woodland garden, home to many treasures and unusual plants. Ron is
a well-known plantsman whose particular passion is trees and shrubs. Many of his
collections have been grown from seeds gathered from all over the world. The garden
is home to a wide variety of bird life, natives and introduced species. The Gordons say
their dawn chorus is better than the radio version! It takes time to see everything here.
*Visits by appointment. Open 1 September to 30 April, Wednesday to Sunday. Plants
for sale. Entry fee. Toilet available.*

The Chittock Family,
"Rosemerryn", R.D.1, Taihape.   Tel:(06) 388 7812
In this extended and revamped garden, many big trees have been underplanted with
azaleas, rhododendrons, perennials and masses of daffodils and tulips. Different areas
are connected by paths and steps. There are also blossom trees, camellias and roses.
Visits by appointment. Toilet available.

Robyn and Joe Woollaston,
"Kiri Kiri Gardens", Moawhango, R.D.2, Taihape.   Tel:(06) 388 1498
Bordering the Moawhango River, and affording delightful views of it, the Woollastons'
garden features an enchanting cottage garden surrounding the house, a native garden
with an island in the river and many flourishing grasses. An intimate bog garden, a
sunken garden and a bold rock garden are other delights. Kiri Kiri, which translates to
'gravel pit' or 'stony place', is a large country garden ideal for a picnic lunch. A
nursery has a wide and varied range of perennials and shrubs.
*Open Wednesday to Sunday, 9 a.m. to 4 p.m., 1 October to 28 February. Tours
welcome. Situated on Burridges Road off Taihape-Napier Road. Entry fee for adults
only. Parking. Toilet.*

Gordon and Annette Collier,
"Titoki Point", R.D.1, Taihape.   Tel:(06) 388 0085
This is a very large and well-known garden, skilfully landscaped and full of interesting and special plantings. Here you will find many rhododendrons, azaleas, magnolias, maples, conifers and camellias, to name just a few of the species. Perennials and
bulbs feature throughout. Of special interest is the great variety of hostas, primulas
and trilliums planted in the wet area at the bottom of a gully where other bog and
shade-loving plants also thrive. This colourful garden needs some time to appreciate.
*Titoki Point is open Wednesday to Sunday, from 10 a.m. to 4 p.m., October to
May. Groups are welcome but please notify of intending visit. Teas and lunches
available by prior arrangement. Campervan facilities. Gordon has a well appointed
nursery where visitors can buy many of the species they see in the garden.*

Owen and Sherie Batley,
"Waitoka", R.D.1, Taihape.   **Tel: (06) 388 7822**
Waitoka Gardens are large country gardens situated 20 km west of Taihape on Ruanui
Road. At 670 metres altitude, Waitoka commands spectacular views of the surrounding countryside and Mount Ruapehu. Sweeping lawns and mature trees provide a
tranquil setting. A collection of native trees attract many wild birds, and the wealth of
plants offers something for every season.

*Open daily from 10 a.m. to 4 p.m. from October to May. Admission $7 season
pass. A selection of plants are available from the plant sales area.*

Manawatu

R. J. D. McKean,
"Torwood", R.D.2, Kimbolton.   **Tel:(06) 328 2705**
This is a pinetum (a large collection of pine species) set out in a large gully with grass
tracks throughout. Some of the species are the only examples in New Zealand, many
having been planted from seed from around the world. Take time to see all the treasures here.
Visits by appointment.

Alan and Ngaire Handcock,
Ruapuna Park and Museum, Rangiwhahia,
R.D.54, Kimbolton.   **Tel:(06) 328 2855**
This property contains 1.4 hectares of park-like gardens with the house section slightly
separate from the main area. One feature is a protected totara tree thought to be around
950 years old. A pond is surrounded by bog plants, and a woodland section is home
to many large-leafed rhododendrons, hostas and the huge *Cardiocrinum giganteum.*
Other beds have mixed collections of rhododendrons, camellia, azaleas and blossom
trees, mostly underplanted with bulbs and ground covers, creating all-year beauty.
Rock gardens with mixtures of specialities and conifers add interest.
*Visits by appointment. Toilet. Small plant nursery. Teas by arrangement. Entry
fee.*

Kimbolton Rhododendron Park,
Haggerty St, Kimbolton.
Occupying a large bank and gully developed, owned and operated by the New Zealand Rhododendron Association, this park features mass plantings of rhododendrons,
azaleas, camellias, conifers, magnolias and blossom trees. A pond at the bottom adds
interest and there are native trees to attract the birds.There are some lovely long vistas

from each end of the park, which offers lots of seats to rest on, as well as picnic tables. Best viewed in spring and early summer.

Open daily. The park is free but there are donation boxes.

Faith and Rodney Wilson,
"Cross Hills Gardens", R.D.54, Kimbolton.
Tel:(06) 328 5797

A 7-hectare country garden, Cross Hills is well known in New Zealand and beyond for its extensive collections of rhododendrons and azaleas. There are around 2000 varieties which flower non-stop from early spring through to summer. Groups of deciduous trees, blossom trees and conifers add interest, and perennials, bulbs and ground covers supply seasonal colour. Visitors will find something of interest throughout the year.

Gardens open to the public. Open every day September to May, 10.30 a.m. to 5 p.m. Entry fee. Coach tours welcome. Ample room for car and coach parking, all large groups please make advance bookings. Tea kiosk open October and November (peak flowering period) for teas, light lunches, film, souvenirs, etc. Open by arrangement for groups during summer and autumn. Picnic tables provided. Toilets available. Please allow time to see this garden. A comprehensive nursery is also open for plant sales from late June through to November. Some of the plants here are only to be found at Cross Hills.

Laurie and Kaye Bradbury,
"Glengarnock", Finnis Rd,
R.D 5, Feilding. **Tel: (06) 328 7726**
A large newly established country garden developed so that views of the expansive rural countryside and Mount Ruapehu to the north can be enjoyed. On a slope, different areas are joined by steps and archways and a croquet lawn is edged with a haha. Cottage plantings comprise a host of old fashioned roses with some modern varieties, lots of self seeding perennials and annuals. Although a colourful garden over spring and summer there is good autumn display due to a mixture of trees.
Visits by appointment. Donation. Picnics welcome. Devonshire teas by arrangement. Situated 24 km from Feilding.

Frances and John McColl,
"Marama", Terrace Road, Kimbolton.
Postal address: R.D.7, Feilding **Tel:(06) 328 5719**
Marama is a large, cottage-style country garden with a backdrop of native bush and a towering river cliff face. The large sweeping beds of rhododendrons, camellias, conifers, roses, natives, bulbs and many perennials encompass expansive lawns. Maple, birch, magnolia, beech, prunus and other trees provide much-needed summer shade. The main area is flat, with a gentle slope planted in a variety of rock and alpine plants. A small pond area is under construction, and with the microclimate here, plantings will be of interest most of the year.
Open weekends October, November and December. Weekday visits by appointment only. Entry fee. Farmhouse accommodation for six

Elspeth and Graeme Shannon,
"Harere", R.D.7, Feilding. **Tel: (06) 328 9754**
This tranquil country garden is designed in a series of enclosed rooms. Features include a number of hedges, heritage roses and perennials. Colour themes are important. A formal vegetable garden is a delightful addition.
Visits by appointment only. Entry fee $4. Buses welcome. Toilet. Situated at Cheltenham Cross Road, 2 minutes from Cheltenham and 20 minutes from famous Cross Hills Kimbolton.

J. and S. Ross,
"Marinoto", Cemetery Road, Sanson. **Tel:(06) 329 3898**
Masses of roses of the modern variety are the predominant flower in this country garden. Collections of miniatures, both standard and bush, and many annuals blend in together. A long drive planted both sides adds a different viewing. Samples of outdoor furniture seen in the garden can be ordered.
Open 7 days all day, October to March. Entry fee.

Ngaire and Geoff Somerville,
"Nikau Farm", Fergusson Road, R.D.9, Feilding **Tel:(06) 328 8726**
This garden has been created on a sloping section which has a deep gully and lovely rural views. The prominent plantings are natives. Ferns, both small and the tree varieties, are all starting to naturalise here. Camellias, with bulbs and perennials, add colour and interest, as do plants of the protea family and roses.
Visits by appointment.

Mr and Mrs A. Mason,
Frank Mason and Son Ltd, Sandon Road, Feilding.   **Tel:(06) 323 5226**
Started in 1912, this is the garden of a leading rose-growing firm and master agent. The nursery and display areas can be viewed during business hours. Mr Mason will give a talk on all aspects of roses: the types, varieties, how to grow and look after them. The company deals in fuchsias as well, and there are major displays here. Purchases can be made.
Open Monday to Saturday, 8.30 a.m. to 4.30 p.m.; closed 12 to 1 p.m. daily, Sundays and statutory holidays. Groups please notify beforehand.

Mount Lees Reserve,
Ngaio Road, Feilding.
This was the home of Mr Ormond Wilson and is now in the care of the Feilding Borough Council. In spring, a large flat area in front of the homestead is a blaze of colour when many thousands of daffodils bloom. The native bush area, which slopes away from the garden, has perennials and bulbs which have naturalised among native ferns and give lots of colour along the walking tracks through spring and summer. A number of exotic trees add interest.
The reserve is open daily from 9 a.m. to 5 p.m. Picnic facilities and toilets available.

Marilyn and Ian Wightman,
"Oranga Plants", Port Street, Feilding.   **Tel/Fax:(06) 323 4233**
Here is a specialist herb display garden set in beds which are mostly in combined colours. Old-fashioned roses blend throughout. The nursery stocks all varieties seen in the garden along with many varieties of perennials, house plants, trees and shrubs.
Open normal business hours.

Kowhai Park,
South St, Feilding.
A delightful park which is tended by the Feilding Borough Council, is noted for its established trees. Various formal rose beds frame a large pond. Over one end, a Japanese-style bridge leads to a large rock garden. A woodland area shelters ferns, rhododendrons and other shade-loving plants.Walking tracks abound. Flower beds have a mixture of perennials, bulbs and annuals. A large aviary is popular with the children.
Accessible daily. Toilets available.

Adrian Ballinger and Eddie Johns,
"O'Tara Birch Gardens", Waitohi Road
P.O. Box 81, Rongotea.   **Tel/Fax:(06) 324 8490**
The theme of this large developing garden is 'gardens of the past for the future', and it is designed formally in rooms and with extensive collections. The dahlia garden is in full glory February to May, the rose garden has over a thousand roses in a knot garden pattern surrounded by beds of climbing and rambling roses over huge pergolas, the maple garden includes a pond, a magnolia lawn, bearded irises and long lawn drive through an avenue of silver birches and a variety of other plantings. A feature throughout the garden's beds are interesting collections of grafted weeping grevilleas. These have been grafted by Adrian and Eddie in their shadehouse. A large lake area features

an extensive Japanese iris collection (peak time for viewing is December). There are other extensions being planned, such as a viewing tower, chess garden and a formal English rose garden.

The gardens are open October/November for bearded irises, December for Japanese irises, January to Easter for dahlias, 10 a.m. to 5 p.m. daily. Entry fee for future development. Plant sales include roses, bearded and Japanese irises, while dahlias can be ordered in summer for delivery in October.

Lynn and Bill Kirkland,
"The Herb Farm", Grove Road, Ashhurst.
Postal: R.D. 10, Palmerston North.   **Tel:(06) 326 8633**
The Herb Farm is a unique concept architecturally, and it was designed for Lynn whose has been interested in medicinal and kitchen herbs for many years. Included in the garden is a delightful children's garden, one for birds, bees and butterflies, a fragrant garden, a formal kitchen garden, medicinal purpose garden, and new developments for a secret garden and picnic areas. The attractive studio is stocked with products from the garden and for Lynn's learning classes, which include cooking and health instruction. A most fascinating 'living wall' forms one wall in the nursery with sections of growing plants, along with potted treasures.

Group tours welcome with talks and demonstrations on herb topics available by arrangement. Mail order catalogue. Plant sales and display gardens open Monday, Wednesday, Saturday and Sunday 1 p.m. to 5 p.m. Other times by appointment.

Dallis and John Sturtevant,
82 Te Awe Awe Street, Palmerston North.   **Tel:(06) 358 0223**
In this large, all-seasons city garden there are two of New Zealand's notable trees: a North American scarlet oak and a kanuka believed to be pre-European. A large collection of old-fashioned roses are at their best in November. Woodland areas feature shade-loving plants, perennials and bulbs. All the flower beds are colour coordinated. The Sturtevants have a collection of outdoor sculptures displayed in different areas of their garden
Visits by appointment.

Dorothy Abraham,
19 Jickell Street, Palmerston North.   **Tel:(06) 358 0117**
Dorothy describes her garden as an 'easy-care small park'. It is a tree and shrub garden, home to two protected trees; a scarlet oak and an English walnut. There are a number of camellias and rhododendrons, and the clematis vines growing up many of the trees give an added dimension to the garden.
Visits by appointment.

Mr and Mrs O.R. O'Neill,
41 Sutherland Crescent, Palmerston North.   **Tel:(06) 357 9922**
Compact planting where the beds of flowers all flow together in a small level city garden are at their best in November and December. Fuchsias, roses, a small pond and waterway, and a variety of climbers add contrast. Many annuals planted twice a year.
Visits by appointment.

Mrs Rona McOviney,
27 Phoenix Ave, Palmerston North.   **Tel:(06) 357 8356**
Sited on a large city section with an interesting terraced area at the back of the garden
and having the Awatea Stream flowing through, forming a sizeable dam at it goes, are
just some of the features of Rona's garden. As a floral artist, many of the numerous
flowers, bulbs, trees and shrubs have been chosen for picking.There are also special
beds of 'picking' flowers planted in suitable varieties for drying and floral work. Many
camellias, roses, azaleas, and perennials blend with natives, conifers and some rhododendrons. A cool covered-in porch is full of potted plants, while a number elsewhere
add to the overall pretty picture.
Visits by arrangement.

Lynne Atkins,
"Greenhaugh", Napier Road, R.D.10, Palmerston North.   **Tel:(06) 357 3878**
Mature trees shelter and frame this large country garden where lawns wander between beds of old-fashioned and David Austin roses, bulbs, self-seeding annuals and
perennials. Statues, a pergola and sunken areas with ponds and rock banks are features in the landscaping. Very colourful spring to autumn. Easy walking.
Open daily except Sunday. Nursery has a large vareity of plants for sale. Entry
fee to garden.

The Esplanade,
Palmerston North.
Bordering the Manawatu River, this garden is very close to the city centre. Native
bush is accessible by many walking tracks; elsewhere, one can drive through the
Esplanade. In the more formal garden complex, a circular area contains a rose garden
with pergolas, a pond and fountain. Another area has tall palms underplanted with
bulbs and annuals in beds of formal design. There are further ponds, large collections
of azaleas, rhododendrons, camellias, cherries, conifers and many other specimen plantings. Perennials, bulbs, annuals and ground covers mix happily everywhere. A large
hothouse and shadehouse complex is open Monday to Friday, 10 a.m. to 12 noon and
1 p.m. to 4 p.m.; Saturday, Sunday and public holidays, 12 noon to 4 p.m. Nearby, a
scented garden nestles under three large cedar trees. A well-appointed children's
playground is another popular feature.
These gardens are all open from dawn to dusk. Toilets available. Gardens are
tended by the Palmerston North City Council.

Ray and Blanche Lauridsen,
"Canaan Camellias", No. 5 R.D.,
Aranui Road, Palmerston North.   **Tel:(06) 329 0879**
Camellias are the speciality in this level country garden surrounded by trees. There
are special ones in a shadehouse and a propagating unit in the garden where the
Lauridsens have successfully grown their own plants. Best time to see is from August
to October.
Visits by appointment. Morning and afternoon teas by arrangement.

Margaret and Jac Bos,
"de Hoeve 23", Aranui Road, R.D.5, Palmerston North. **Tel:(06) 329 0704**
This established English-designed garden has been added to and now includes many
roses (old world and modern), camellias, cottage garden perennials, pergolas, ponds
and bridges. A native bush area has been planted. An easy-walking all-year garden.
Old World roses and cottage plants for sale.
Visits by appointment. Toilet available. Morning & afternoon teas by arrangement.

Ngaire and Bruce Cheetham,
"Kauwhata", Rangitikei Line,
R.D.5, Palmerston North. **Tel: (06) 357 1352**
A country cottage garden with roses, old and new, and perennials surrounding the 76-
year-old home. The recent introduction of the Secret Garden walkway, winds its way
down the length of the drive.
Visits by appointment.

Zetta and Noel Robertson,
65 Ruamahanga Crescent, Palmerston North. **Tel:(06) 357 7524**
In this small, intensively planted city garden the emphasis is on perennials. These are
combined with a large collection of bulbs, alpines and ground covers. Zetta also

grows camellias. Other trees, such as cherry, add to the beauty, and there are also roses, orchids and many ferns. With so many treasures flowering all year round, this is a real collector's garden.
Visits by appointment.

Sue and Ian McKelvie,
"Pukemarama", R.D.3, Palmerston North   **Tel:(06) 324 8446**
A very large long-established garden, Pukemarama is formally laid out along English lines. Areas are now being revamped by Sue. Most of the trees were originally planted in pairs. The front of the section is very steep and is completely terraced in brick. Roses, mostly modern varieties, feature throughout the garden. A woodland area, known as the dell, contains mature trees underplanted with camellias, rhododendrons, azaleas, perennials and bulbs.
Open Sunday and Monday only during October and November, 10 a.m. to 5 p.m. Coachloads by appointment all year. Entry fee. Morning and afternoon teas can be supplied by arrangement. Toilet available. Visitors are welcome to bring their own lunch and picnic on the vast lawn.

Note: *Through the Pahiatua-Ackautere Road is the garden of R. Abraham. This is only 20 minutes from Palmerston North. See the listing for the Wairarapa.*

Levin Botanical Gardens, Kent Street, Levin.
These occupy a large level area of land near the shopping centre. On one side, bordering Kent Street, are the rose gardens, where formal beds of one colour create a mass display during late spring and summer, and lines of standards are combined with archways covered in climbing roses. The rest of the garden is notable for several features: the Cenotaph surrounded by a large rock garden; a long shallow lily pond; a delightful sunken paved walkway with lots of hanging plants; and a scented garden. A begonia house, full of tender tropical plants and flowers, is open for viewing between 9 a.m. and 3 p.m. weekdays. Probably the most prominent area is the garden that surrounds historic Thompson House. A well-grown collection of native trees has paths wandering through and lots of shade-loving plants beneath. Camellias, rhododendrons, azaleas and roses are also found in this old-world garden. Thompson House may be hired. Contact (06) 368 7689 or (06) 368 5023 to view.
Accessible daily.

Ivan and Pat Keating,
"Buttercup Acres", Florida Road, Ohau, Levin.   **Tel:(06) 368 0557**
Surrounded by a belt of alders for shelter, this large, recently developed country garden (1989) is easy walking and has all-year interest through its large collection of rhododendrons, camellias, flowering cherries, magnolias, perennials, daffodils and bulbs, not forgetting numerous varieties of lilac, birches and conifers. Also featuring is a large pond supporting bird life, surrounding paddocks that are home to miniature horses and delightful alpacas, whose babies are born December to March. A small shop sells gifts made from alpaca fibre.
Open Wednesday to Sunday including public holidays, 10 a.m. to 6 p.m. Monday and Tuesday by appointment only. Entry fee.

A. H. Guy,
"Kereru", Koputaroa Road, R.D. 5, Levin.   **Tel:(06) 368 7581**
In this large flat garden, surrounding an historic house, are various well-grown 60-year-old trees, including a collection of magnolias. A registered tree, the *Magnolia denudata* or Yulan tree, is a magnificent sight in spring. There are camellias and some clematis, which are literally climbing everywhere. Occasional flower beds add interest and contrast; these contain herbaceous plants and roses.
Visits by appointment. Entry fee.

George and Beatrice Gimblet,
Gladstone Road, Levin.   **Tel:(06) 368 7321**
The backdrop of native bush, Waiopehu Reserve, gives depth and contrast to this large, gently sloping country garden. The garden has a comprehensive collection of rhododendrons, mollis and evergreen azaleas and camellias. Wide grass walkways wind throughout the curving planted areas. Hostas and other damp- and shade-loving plants edge the bush, along with large-leafed rhododendrons. A delightful walk meanders through the bush and ends with four majestic redwoods, one having been planted in 1895, the others in 1942. Low-growing conifers fill a long bed at one side of the house, while others are raised beds of mixed plantings. Bird life is plentiful.
Visits by appointment. Picnics on the lawn welcome for groups.

Mr and Mrs L. A. McKelvie,
"Aysgarth", R.D.1, Levin.   **Tel:(06) 368 7461**
The emphasis is on roses in this large rural garden. Miniatures, bush and patio varieties are grown, some in formal gardens and others under shelter for showing purposes; Aysgarth's owners have had some success in this area in the past.
Visits by appointment

Mary and Deane Robertson,
"Serenity", S.H.1, Manakau, R.D.31, Levin.   **Tel:(06) 362 6869**
As you enter the garden, the rockery dominates the scene. Drenched by sun all day, the gentle rolling slope is ideal for little treasures. A dry stone wall borders the rockery and provides the background for the perennial border. This border is a jumble of flowers and foliage during the summer months, all billowing and spilling over each other, clamouring for centre stage. Old world roses arch and preen gracefully above the chaos. The border stretches some 100 metres to the northern boundary and parts of it are grouped into separate colours; it is broken up by two pergolas. The larger of the two supports *Wisteria floribunda macrobotrys* which is a flowering stream of scented chains during October. Through this you reach 'Tranquillity', a garden of light and shade, of space and enclosure. Stretch your legs up the gentle slope that leads you to the Eastern bank. This is a garden of trees and water, and promise. Features include the 'Mt Fuji Tunnel' and the 'Helleborous Hillock'. Recent additions are a lake totally planted in natives. The vision has been to create a garden of recreation, education and inspiration; and somewhere for people to stretch their legs, perhaps picnic on the lawn under trees, view a wide range of plant material to inspire would-be gardeners. Entrance to Serenity Garden is via Pukehou Nursery.
Open 10 a.m. daily 1st August to 31st March. Entry fee for adults, children free. Toilets. Complimentary tea and coffee. Friends of Serenity: special buying privileges, garden workshops, regular newsletters, entry to garden all year.

A.M. and M. L. Turnbull,
"Talisman Nurseries Ltd", Ringawhati Road,
R.D. Otaki.   Tel:(06) 364 5893/Fax:(06)364 5893
This nursery specialises in native trees and plants. Many of the species seen here are rare or unusual. A large flat area is planted out with everything from canopy trees to the small shrubby varieties so visitors can see each species to its best advantage. A rock and alpine bed is also well landscaped. Alongside, set in a tree-developed area, are probably the oldest brick stables in this region.
Open during usual business hours. Group visits welcome but prior notice would be appreciated.

Cynthia and Bruce Coe,
"Coehaven", 150 Rangiuru Road, Otaki.   Tel:(06) 364 7001
A fair share of native trees have been used at Coehaven for shelter, garden divisions and framing areas. Close by the coast where the salt winds play havoc, many proteas, conifers and camellias have grown well as do the predominant specialities, European heathers and South African ericas. Raised flower beds edge the expansive lawns where these favourites can be seen to their best advantage, blending with fuchsias, azaleas and a variety of small shrubs. Statues dot the gardens and there are a number of resting spots where the vistas can be seen. The formally designed rose gardens and wide steps add to the enjoyment. Many of the flowers in the garden are prized for floral work.
Nursery and nursery gardens open, Friday and Saturday, 9 a.m. to 4.30 p.m. Closed Easter and Christmas to New Year. Theatre readings and seminars combined with tours of the private gardens of Coehaven by arrangement (min. 20 people, max. 50).

Ann and Graham Carthew,
"Ngawai Farm", Corbetts Road, Otaki.   Tel:(06) 364 7462
Landscaped in a gully using the natural contours and with a small water flow winding down through the garden forming a series of ponds as it goes, this large coastal garden has lovely sea views in the distance. Plantings are mixtures of conifers, natives, camellias, blossom and deciduous trees. Many pets enjoy the tranquillity, along with a young family. Spring brings daffodils on the expansive lawns and flower beds are full of roses and perennials. Bog plants edge the waterways. Seats, bridges, steps and walkways to help the visitor enjoy this garden.
Visits by appointment. Entry fee.

David and Jacqui Pritchard,
Forest Lakes Road, Otaki.   Tel:(06) 364 5123 or 364 7292
The Pritchards' large woodland country garden has an equally large natural lake edged on one side by a stand of native bush, home to many water birds. One side of the garden has been planted in masses of rhododendrons, camellias and deciduous trees edged with native trees. Paths wind throughout, while a platform enables visitors to view the serenity of the lake and its reflections. Behind the house is a steep sand hillside planted in proteas, flaxes and natives giving all-year colour. Elsewhere low-growing conifers, roses and other shrubs fill easy-care beds.
Visits by appointment. Entry fee.

Hugh and Helen Guthrie,
"Totara Grove", Old Hautere Road, Otaki.   **Tel:(06) 364 3394**
An endless supply of stones from the property have been used for edging pathways all
through a stand of native bush next to this large level country garden. Totaras dominate and a glade in the centre of the bush has camellias and golden elms planted
around a semi-circle while the other sides have numerous rhododendrons, camellias,
hostas and other shade plants adding an interesting contrast. Elsewhere in the garden
there are many, many David Austin roses in flower beds, over archways and along a
long colonnade. Modern roses, clipped box hedges, deciduous and blossom trees,
and potted plants make up this all-year garden. Many of the flowers in the garden are
used for Helen's pot-pourri.
Visits by appointment. Entry fee. Roses and plants for sale.

"Glorious Otaki Gardens"

*The following four gardens can be seen together and can arrange teas and lunches
for groups.*

Betsy and Neil Bruere,
"Ballantrae", 117 Rangiuru Road, Otaki.   **Tel:(06) 364 6158**
Developed on a large level coastal section in rooms with a small water pond in a low
depression and many varieties of trees, Ballantrae has flower beds of perennials, roses,
a vegetable patch and orchard. Quite a wide variety of plantings and damp and shade
plants edge the water area, while a thick wood of natives forms a backdrop on one
side, where mass plantings of Chatham Island forget-me-nots can be viewed. Bridges,
arches and seats add character.
Visits by appointment. Toilet.

Lloyd and Ann Chapman,
"Trinity Farm", Waitohu Valley Road, Otaki.   **Tel/Fax: (06) 364 6193**
Roses are the main feature in this level country garden, designed in a semi-formal
English style with box hedging, raised beds, long rose walks and archways. A new
area is being developed and combines the use of lavender beds, a pond and masses of
perennials. An extensive nursery is stocked with all varieties of classical roses. Mail
order catalogue available. Seminars are held regularly on the care of the rose.
Picnics welcome. Open 7 days during daylight. Toilet.

Mary and David Williams,
"Rangimarie", Te Roto Road, Otaki.   **Tel:(06) 364 5144**
Translated, Rangimarie means 'peace and harmony', whch is immediately felt in this
woodland garden, dominated by an immense pohutukawa tree, round which the Japa-
nese-style house was built and where all windows enjoy wonderful garden views.
Other features include a pond, sunken herb garden, hedge of *Camellia* 'Bellbird',
expansive sweeping lawns and a comprehensive collection of Bonsai trees.
Entry fee. Toilet. Visits by appointment.

Nanette and Tom Milburn,
"Stoney Broak", Gorge Road, Otaki.   **Tel:(06) 364 3200**
Being an expert embroiderer, the artistic flair shows in Nanette's level country garden. Sweeping lawns are set off with curving beds of massed perennials and old-fashioned roses. The rare and unusual can be seen throughout and all the beds are colour co-ordinated. Trees and shrubs, along with many natural-growing totara, shelter the section. Free-flying doves enjoy the tranquillity. The attractive nursery is set off by a long bed of hot colours and a display of colourful perennials. A shop sells handmade gifts.
   Donation to Save the Children. Visits by appointment.

Kapiti Coast/ Wellington

Mary and Robert Burnard,
"Burnard Gardens", R.D. Waikanae.   **Tel:(04) 293 3371**
This large, level rural garden has 7 different garden areas. A formal section features a
sunken waterlily pond and 60-m double herbaceous borders, beyond which a 40-m
pergola is covered with wisteria, roses and hybrid clematis. There is also a woodland
garden, planted with rhododendrons, azaleas, bluebells, lilies and wild flowers, a vegetable garden and herb garden, an old-fashioned rose garden and a bush walk alongside the Waikanae River. .
Open Sunday from 10 a.m. to 4 p.m., 1 October to 31 March. Groups 20+ and
wedding ceremonies on other days by arrangement only. Self-contained twin ac-
commodation available in separate guest quarters.

Irene and Cliff Chillingworth,
"Blue Heron Gardens", 39 Greenaway Road, Waikanae. Tel:(04) 293 6099
 A wide variety of high-limbed, mature trees shelter and let dappled light through to
this large, urban, coastal woodland garden that has a comprehensive collection of
rhododendrons, camellias and azaleas among its plantings. Interesting landscaping
has resulted in delightful resting corners, rooms and dells. Water ponds, local stones,
curved grass walkways, steps, archways and an area of modern rose beds add to the
charm, along with damp bog areas and the coloured bark of the tall eucalyptus trees.
Collections of native trees and a wide variety of South African and Australian species
can also be seen.
Visitors welcome all year by appointment. Entry fee.

Joy and Vern Darke,
7 Hurunui St., Waikanae.   **Tel:(04) 293 5874**
The house and garden in this level urban section have been designed in harmony so
views of garden areas from inside the house can be enjoyed. Tall natural-growing
kohekohe trees have lent maturity to the other plantings, which include a fine collection of camellias, many deciduous trees which produce good autumn colour, magnolias, some rhododendrons and a selection of natives. Foliage plantings are important
to Joy so there are lots of perennials and ground covers which help make up this all-
year garden. A host of native birds can be seen and heard. A herb and vegetable patch
is also attractive. Stones which have been dug out of the ground while the garden was
being developed have been used for pathways.
Visits by appointment all year. Entry fee.

Margaret Eaton,
"Rose Cottage", 55 Park Ave, Waikanae.   **Tel:(04) 293 4679**
Colourful is the scene all year in this small, coastal, urban section where the flower
beds are massed with a wide range of cottage plants and old-fashioned roses. Trees
and shrubs are kept pruned so as not to overshadow the predominantly soft colour-
coordinated curving beds. Potted plants and climbers add contrast.
Visits by appointment. Entry fee.

Graham and June Humphrey,
"Greenmantle", Main Road North, Paraparaumu.   **Tel:(04) 298 6545**
A large rural garden on a sloping section, Greenmantle is noted for its established
trees, including oaks, beeches, ginkgos, rhododendrons, camellias and azaleas. In
spring, the ground beneath is massed with daffodils. There are plantings of roses,
vireya rhododendrons and geraniums, and native bush backing onto the section attracts birds.
Visits by appointment.

Raewyn and Denzil Philp,
"Springhill Gardens", 91 Muri Road, Pukerua Bay.   **Tel:(04) 239 9148**
Being a floral artist's garden, much of the plantings at Springhill can be used for this
purpose. White is a favourite colour and throughout all the flower beds it is mixed
with mainly colour-coordinated perennials, roses, bulbs, ground covers, blossom trees,
wisterias and shrubs. A long bed of 'Iceberg' standard roses and lavender makes a
delightful entrance and a long wide pergola has white roses and wisterias climbing
over it, while the base is planted in ivy and geraniums. As this is a country garden on
the edge of suburbia, the aim is to keep a country flavour. A formal paved garden is in
the development stages. Prime time for viewing is in summer.
Visits by appointment.

The Old Porirua Cemetery, Kenepuru Drive, Porirua.
Because of the age of this cemetery — as far back as the 1870s — the design was
causing maintenance problems for the Porirua City Council, and the decision was
made to develop a garden effect. Stone banks and walls hold the slipping edges and
grass walkways separate grave lines. Rhododendrons have been planted throughout
and masses of perennials and small shrubs fill old grave sites, and spill over to delightful effect. It is easy walking and close to the city centre.

Gear Homestead, Whitford Brown Ave, Porirua.
This garden surrounds an historic house now administered by the Porirua City Council. Plantings are mixed. Some of the large pine trees were planted at the beginning of development and there is a lot of regenerating native flora throughout. The collections of camellias, roses and perennials in flower beds, local stone walls, small trimmed hedges and wide sweeping lawns are a delight to wander round.
The gardens are accessible at all times. Toilets available. The Homestead is open to the public on the first Sunday of each month, 1 p.m. to 5 p.m., or by arrangement. It can also be booked for social functions. Telephone Porirua City Council, (04) 237 5089, or Gear Homestead, (04) 237 8540, for further details.

The next two gardens may be visited at the same time.

Phillida and David Weaver,
"Pepped Warbeck Gardens",
660 Ohariu Valley Road, Johnsonville.   **Tel:(04) 478 7586**
A large peaceful country garden surrounded by rolling farmland. It's a garden for all seasons, full of old fashioned roses and unusual plants and trees. Extending to 4½ acres overall it consists of many separate areas, each dedicated to a particular theme and inter-connected by brick archways, paths, tree lined walks, hedges and steps. The sculpture-like form of a large macrocarpa is of particular interest. A recent development is a large bog garden. Most plants seen in the garden are for sale.
Visits by appointment. Entry fee. Phillida holds garden seminars at advertised times. Teas by arrangement, plenty of room if weather unfavourable. Bed and breakfast accommodation for 2.

Suzy and Mark Pennington,
"Sudbury", 60 Takarau Gorge Road,
Ohariu Valley, Johnsonville.   **Tel:(04) 478 4846**
A predominant feature at Sudbury is a lake, with an island, in front of the house fed by a natural stream. A walking track winds all around and a hump bridge enables access to the island. An extensive collection of rhododendrons behind the lake has peonies, camellias and natives among its plantings. Features include a magnolia walk, underplanted with masses of pink tulips, a courtyard sheltering subtropical species, a wisteria tunnel, a long, tree-lined drive, edged with agapanthus, and a hazelnut grove.
Visits by appointment. Entry fee.

Wellington Botanic Garden, Lady Norwood Rose Garden,
Access from Tinakori Road, Glenmore St or Upland Road, City.
Spreading over hills, valleys and flattish land above the central city, this park of around 26 hectares has much to offer the garden lover. The terrain in many areas dictates the design and appropriate plantings. Woodland gardens shelter in small valleys under various canopy trees, along with a mixture of native and exotic trees, often underplanted with rhododendrons, azaleas, hostas, lilies, fuchsias and hydrangeas. Tree ferns also grow throughout. A small stream cascades into a pond at one point, where

landscaping focuses on water-loving species. Elsewhere, one finds a herb garden and steep rock gardens full of cacti, succulents, low-growing plants and ground covers. Formally laid out flower beds are usually filled with bulbs, such as tulips, for spring and annuals for the months following. A network of paved paths and steps or well-formed tracks link the various gardens in the park, which also has many large lawn areas. Some of these are used for sports. A well equipped children's playground is here, too.

The **Lady Norwood Rose Garden** is on a sheltered plateau, where a circular area has been laid out in formal rose beds, each one containing a different colour and variety, some 104 in all. Surrounding three sides is a large semicircular colonnade of bricks over which roses climb vigorously. Backing these rose gardens is a large complex containing a begonia house and a restaurant. Filled with tender plants, some potted, some in hanging baskets and others ground grown, the conservatory has delightful displays which change with the seasons. Plants range from ferns, popular potted flowers, orchids and begonias to many tropical 'specials' such as bougainvilleas, hibiscus, frangipanis and gardenias. The Tea House provides light meals and snacks in a conservatory-styled setting. The above complex is open from 10 a.m. to 4 p.m. daily.

At the city end of the gardens is the **Bolton Street Memorial Park,** site of one of the city's earliest cemeteries. This park could be described now as a very colourful 'living cemetery', for here mature trees shelter many old roses, perennials and naturalised bulbs. There are seats tucked in quiet corners and this part of the park is used by walkers, joggers, shoppers and city workers alike.

Accessible daily.

Otari Native Botanic Garden,
Wilton Road, Wellington.

This famous garden of native flora was developed from an original piece of bushland. There are species from all over New Zealand and the aim is to preserve for future generations living examples of our flora showing how it can be used for landscaping purposes, whether it be on a large scale or just in the average domestic garden. At Otari, there are many defined gardens featuring fern, grass and sedge, rock, alpine, flax and hebe species. Examples throughout are named and their place of origin is noted. The paths are gravelled in this truly native garden. It is a must for anyone interested in New Zealand's flora.

Accessible daily. Picnic places, toilets and a water tap available.

Bob and Jo Munro,
"Moss Green Garden", R.D.2, Akatarawa, Upper Hutt.   Tel:(04) 526 7531

Sitting on a bridge looking down at the clear-flowing Akatarawa River or walking along the boulders in the river bed looking up at a huge *Magnolia campbellii* and large-leaf rhododendrons are just some of the delightful treats in this tranquil woodland garden, where exotic plantings are completely in harmony with the surrounding native bush. A wide range of plants are grown; there is a small stream forming ponds edged with damp-loving plants, roses over fences, archways, and many, many perennials, bulbs and ground covers. The unusual is to be seen everywhere. There is something exciting in the garden all year round, although it is at its best from October to May. There are masses of birds and good autumn colour.

Open 6 days. Closed Tuesdays, except holidays or by appointment. Closed June and July except by appointment. Entry fee. Discount for groups. Visitors are welcome to picnic. Large nursery sells comprehensive range of plants. Classes are held during autumn and winter on various aspects of gardening.

Shirley and Ernest Crosgrove,
"Efildoog Sculpture Farm", 1995 Akatarawa Road,
R.D.2, Upper Hutt. **Tel:(04) 526 7924**

Spelling 'good life' in reverse, this very large country garden set amongst tall native trees, has the Akatarawa River flowing through, and an extensive collection of rhododendrons, the large leafed, tiny and species varieties. Other plantings include camellias, magnolias and a great many others including *Prunus.* The unusual feature is a number of sculptures throughout, placed with the long vista ahead. Other interesting aspects are a pond with trout, a waterway edged in bog plants, a clematis-covered gazebo, box hedging, use of local stone on steps, banks and garden designs, a Bonsai collection and Hyper tufa pots. There are also wide sweeping lawns, steps and a swing bridge. Although a blaze of colour in spring, there is also good autumn colour. There have been 35 species of birds sighted in the garden and free-flying doves enjoy it too. The inclusion of an art gallery is planned, housing a display of early NZ original paintings. A sculptor will be actively working in the garden during summer.

Garden open 9.a.m. to 5 p.m., spring and summer. Entry fee.

Vogel House,
75 Woburn Road, Lower Hutt.

A 0.9-hectare garden and lawn surrounds Vogel House, the official residence of the Prime Minister of New Zealand. Some very large trees feature and in recent years quite a collection of natives has been added to the plantings. Flower beds are planted out with annuals, perennials and lilies. There are collections of rhododendrons, camellias, azaleas and blossom trees. Roses predominate in the summer. Immaculately trimmed hedges and shaped trees feature.

For information, apply in writing c/o Prime Minister's Office, Parliament Buildings, Wellington.

Riddiford Gardens,
Mertle St, Lower Hutt.

Close to the city centre, these large public gardens are noted for their many mature shade trees and brilliant beds of annuals. A stream here is crossed by several bridges and there is a pond with a fountain. Numerous large, formally laid out gardens, mass planted with annual bedding plants, make a striking display in spring and summer. Within the gardens, the Gibbes Watson Conservatory houses many tender potted plants. Adjacent is the Tutukiwi Orchid and Fern House. These are open from 10 a.m. to 4 p.m. on weekends and public holidays.

Accessible daily and cared for by the Lower Hutt City Council.

Mitchell Park,
Mitchell Street, Lower Hutt.

This is a large level area set out in formal rose gardens. Each bed is planted in one colour, creating a dramatic effect. Shade trees are dotted throughout the expansive lawns. Another garden in the care of the Lower Hutt City Council.

Accessible daily.

Christine and Gerald Curran,
"L'Amour Coastal Garden", Coast Road,
Orongorongo, Wainuiomata.   **Tel:(04) 564 8323**
Situated on the coast facing the rugged Cook Strait with all its blustery salt winds, this
delightful garden has been developed on a 0.6-hectare level section in the form of
rooms, each with interesting seating arrangements. Local stones have been used in
landscaping walls, banks, pillars and archways. Cottage plants feature on one side
while hardier varieties, such as South African proteas, grow elsewhere. Glassed-in
gazebos are placed where views of the sea, arid hills and garden vistas can be enjoyed.
As the name suggests, this garden has been a labour of love, and from a difficult site
a viable microclimate has been created.

*Groups by appointment please. Visiting September to May, Thursday and Friday,
and Sunday all year round, 11 a.m. to 4 p.m. Toilet. Entry fee. Devonshire teas and
lunches. Picnics welcome. Plants for sale.*

Christine and Dale Hoy,
"Catchpool Country Garden",
Coast Road, Wainuiomata.   **Tel:(04) 564 3637**
This is a large relaxing country garden, with easy walking and interest all year. Entry
is through a stand of tall native trees which extends along three sides of the garden,
underplanted with a host of rhododendrons and many leafy species. It is all pathed,
and paths are lined with rengarenga lilies. Extensive lawns feature conifers, perennial
beds, some roses and many deciduous trees. Native birds abound and Dale says the
dawn chorus is wonderful.

Entry fee. Picnics welcome. Open most days. Teas and lunches by arrangement.

Imogene and Tim Keenan,
"Hillcrest", 20 Hair Street, Wainuiomata.   **Tel:(04) 564 6408**
As a floral artist, Imogene has developed her colourful, small, split level, romantic
garden so she can pick flowers and foliage all year. Designed in rooms, such as the
medieval 'room' complete with bell tower, roses and herbs with matching names, the
Gothic and the cottage, Tim's construction works complement the garden and potted
plantings.

*Garden open Sundays, 11.am. to 4 p.m. mid November to end of April. A speciality
at Hillcrest are medieval coffee and dessert evenings. Monday to Friday inclusive, 7
p.m. to 9 p.m. Large groups welcome with a minimum of 6, advanced reservations
needed, mid December to mid March.*

David and Verona Lewis,
"Rosecroft", 965 Coast Rd,
R.D.1, Wainuiomata.   **Tel: (04) 564 5918**
A rhododendron garden with approximately 200 varieties (250 bushes in all); also
camellias and Heritage roses. There is a raised stone walled pond with goldfish and
water lilies, with gunnera featuring as a backdrop. There is a bog garden with cande-
labra primulas and gunnera etc. The garden is just over an acre and fairly new, and is
still being developed. It has numerous gravel pathways to all parts of the garden.
Access to the property is rather steep, but there is parking for approximately twelve
cars. However, buses would not be able to negotiate a sharp corner.

Only open by appointment in spring and early summer.

Dorothy Archibald and Bill Walker,
"Glen Ferny", 24 Moana Road, Days Bay, Eastbourne.　　Tel:(04) 562 7202
This large urban garden on a steep slope has a backdrop of native trees, and is home to many birds. This bush offers an interesting walk on a track where, at various corners, the view over the bay is delightful. Plantings are mixtures of flowering trees and shrubs, particularly rhododendrons, camellias, azaleas and magnolias. Roses, perennials, bulbs and ground covers provide interesting contrast and colour.
Visits by appointment.

NEW ZEALAND GARDENING BOOKS FROM DAVID BATEMAN LIMITED

Bateman New Zealand Growers Handbooks

Azalea Growers Handbook	Geoff Bryant	$24.95
Bougainvillea Growers Handbook	Jan Iredell	$24.95
Camellia Growers Handbook	Margaret Tapley	$24.95
Container Gardening	Janet Cheriton	$24.95
David Austin's English Roses	Barbara Lea Taylor	$24.95
Flower Growers Handbook	Geoff Bryant	$24.95
Gardens for Free	Geoff Bryant	$24.95
Greenhouse Gardening	Geoff Bryant	$24.95
Herb Growers Handbook	GeoffBryant	$24.95
Old-fashioned Roses	Barbara Lea Taylor	$24.95
Orchid Growers Handbook	I.D. James	$24.95
Organic Gardening	Moira Ryan	$24.95
Protea Growers Handbook	Lew Matthews	$24.95
Rhododendron Growers Handbook	Margaret Tapley	$24.95
Rose Growers Handbook	Janet Cheriton	$24.95
Scented Plants	Margaret Liddell	$24.95
Vegetable Growers Handbook	T.W. Walker	$24.95

New Zealand Gardening Books from David Bateman Limited

Bateman Good Gardening Guides

Growing Bougainvilleas	Jan Iredell	$29.95
Growing Orchids	I.D. James	$29.95
Growing Plants for Free	Geoff Bryant	$29.95
Growing Rhododendrons & Azaleas	Geoff Bryant	$29.95
Growing Roses	Janet Cheriton	$29.95
Growing Camellias	Margaret Tapley	$29.95
Growing Miniature & Patio Roses	D. & B. Eagle	$29.95
Growing Old-fashioned Roses	B. Lea Taylor	$29.95

**These titles are available through
all good bookstores.**

NEW ZEALAND GARDENING BOOKS FROM DAVID BATEMAN LIMITED

General Gardening Books

A Book of Gardens	Anthony/Hanly	$44.95
Complete New Zealand Gardener	Scarrow/Bryant	$49.95
Creating a Natural Garden in NZ	Jacob DeRuiter	$39.95
Gardens in the Wind	Jacob DeRuiter	$29.95
Gardens to Visit in NZ (combined)	Alison McRae	$29.95
Gardens to Visit Upper North Island	Alison McRae	$12.95
Gardens to Visit Lower North Island	Alison McRae	$12.95
Gardens to Visit South Island	Alison McRae	$12.95
Growing New Zealand Plants, Trees and Shrubs	Fisher/Forde	$59.95
Town & Country Gardens	Hanly/Matthews	$44.95
Ultimate NZ Gardening Book	Geoff Bryant (ed.)	$89.95
Ultimate Book of Flowers	Geoff Bryant (ed.)	$89.95
Rare and Unusual Plants	Geoff Bryant	$39.95
Favourite Roses for New Zealand	Peter Harkness	$39.95
Creative New Zealand Gardening	Janet Cheriton	$44.95